W. Lawrence Lipton
presents

—

Death Over Life
Secret of Revelation
A Prophecy of American Destruction

W. Lawrence Lipton
presents

Death Over Life
Secret of Revelation
A Prophecy of American Destruction

Copyright © 2014

Books may be ordered through booksellers or by contacting:

www.createspace.com/4727887
www.Amazon.com

Jacked Design by Guebres Studios

ISBN-13: 978-1497427167 (sc)
ISBN-10: 1497427169 (ebk)

Printed in the United States of America
CreateSpace rev. date: 04/01/2014

You feel Guilty

The Book of Revelation distinguishes between those who are Jews, those who claim to be Jews – but are not – and gentiles. Your approach to feeling guilty might well reveal which you are, and how you will do on the supposed Judgement Day.

As a general rule, Jews usually feel guilty for not doing enough. They function on the basis that they could have done more, they should have done more, and maybe would have done more if they hadn't been distracted. The Jewish attitude is that all things are universally held, and that, if one has more than another, it is because they are holding it in trust for the other, are exercising a form of stewardship over communal property.

Gentiles feel guilty about what they have actually done. They are ashamed of their urges or deeply rooted feelings. When it comes to providing for others, often they feel they are doing too much – dismiss any further action as 'socialist'.

Those who claim to be Jews, but are not, assert their belief and reliance upon the Jewish texts which proclaim stewardship over communal property, but act in a very selfish, or Gentile, manner.

The Qur'an [3:81-82] states:

"God took a pledge from the prophets, saying, 'If, after I have bestowed Scripture and wisdom upon you, a messenger comes confirming what you have been given, you must believe in him and support him. Do you affirm this and accept My pledge as binding on you?' They said, 'We do.' He said, 'Then bear witness and I too will bear witness.' Those who turn away after this are the ones who break pledges."

But who feels guilty violating a pledge cited in the Qur'an?

CHAPTERS

Prologue – Prophecy

I love prophecy. It expresses in a mystical fashion that which is observable and predicable in a historical or scientific context.

If you recognize that human psychology is always consistent, but that technology is constantly changing, the philosophy behind the idea of prophecy takes on a slightly different perspective. If you then add the fact that certain people – those who might be termed as dyslexic, autistic, or experiencing any number of perceptional variations once classified as being 'possessed by spirits or demons', but now seen as statistically normal behavior or learning disorders – see the world differently, and sub-consciously make connections which are highly accurate yet inexplicable without the benefit of a detailed examination of facts beyond the normal range of daily observation.

There is a tendency not to think beyond the simplistic blame game approach which characterized early human life and culture. That blame game consisted of the basic idea and practice: "If you don't understand the cause, then blame it on some deity." If things go well, than the gods are smiling on you; if they should go well, but something ridiculous, or statistically improbable happens, than it is clear that Loki or some other gamester deity is having fun at your expense.

If you are dealing with someone who is a simpleton – or who you perceive to be too dim-witted, or too young, to comprehend things – you blow off the explanation with a magical creature. Or you might invoke that magical being to create fear and thus invoke an obedient response: A child loses their baby teeth so the Tooth Fairy will come and give them money; the sandman comes when you sleep, so you wake with crystals in your eyes; Lady Luck smiles on you when you gamble and win, but turns her back on you when you lose; behave or the bogeyman will get you; behave or you'll go to Hell.

Then there is the great Flip Wilson line, "The Devil made me do it." We see a portion of society who routinely invoke the devil as a justification for their actions – Islamic Jihadists habitually invoke their desire to destroy "the Great Satan," as a justification for their practice of suicide-bomber-murder; for Christians it has always been a motive for the torture, or burning alive, of those they oppose. But neither ever thinks through their logic, or the basis for it.

Over the past thirty-five years, those who have read my books know that I have no problem with their being a GOD – and that I might rethink that belief, if someone could explain how we got something from nothing (how the universe came into existence) in the absence of something which meets the fundamental definition of a Creator Deity, or a 'self-begotten beginning'.

Biblical prophecy is based upon Hebrew traditions and those traditions must be recognized. The Book of Revelation talks to those who willfully, often with malice, violate the traditional Laws they proclaim sacred. Rami b. Hama said: A wild beast has no dominion over man unless he appears to it as a brute, for it is written. Men are overruled when they appear as beasts. The Book of Revelation describes that which will befall humanity as a series of beasts.

The Book of Revelation speaks of seven Angels who will spill vials of the wrath of god; if we think of this in terms of the Garden of Eden and the serpent, the scriptural concept is one which depicts divine agents interacting with humanity to achieve an objective.

In the Garden, Adam is told to eat only fruit; then he receives a commandment not to eat fruit from one specific plant – the Tree of Knowledge. Our logical problem arises from the idea that the Creator is All-knowing and All-Wise, which infers that He should have known Adam would eat from the Tree. But Adam went about his assigned tasks and avoided the fruit – he displayed no desire to acquire knowledge, or improve himself in any way.

Having created a species which was blindly obedient, the Creator then introduces a variation – Eve – who actually thinks and reasons. Then the Serpent is introduced as a resident of the Tree.

Hebrew Midrash tells us that the Serpent reasoned with Eve, and pointed out that he was able to eat the fruit without any adverse affect – therefore it was unlikely that either she, or Adam, "would surely die" if they ate it.

> "When the woman saw that the fruit of the tree was good for food and pleasing to the eye, and also desirable for gaining wisdom, she took some and ate it." [Genesis 3:6]

Understanding the logic and evidence, Eve tries the Apple and discovers it tastes good. But more importantly she suffers no ill-effects and so brings the fruit to Adam. Suddenly there is a transformation in their thinking and they understand the concept of nudity – but they also acquire the knowledge and means to make clothes. More important, *THEY DO NOT DIE.* The Serpent was telling the truth, and the Creator had misrepresented reality.

Now some would say that, eventually, Adam did die. But that means they did not read the story of Noah, and did not learn that only those who carried divine genetics had eternal life – Adam is a divine image, an icon; he certainly is not an entity who is of divine ancestry – therefore he was not created with eternal life. Adam was created from dust and clay, he was the first Golem.

In the Talmud (Sanhedrin 38b), Adam was initially created as a Golem when his dust was "kneaded into a shapeless husk."

A Golem is a Jewish "monster" which serves as the model for what would eventually become the Greek Prometheus (one of the Titans, whose name means "forethought"), and then, in 1818, would enter modern mythology as Mary Shelly's Frankenstein Monster.

In reality, Adam was created as a mindless clay animation, whereas the Serpent was presented in the same role it held in every non-Hebrew culture – a symbol, accompanied by a Tree and female, of the wisdom, knowledge and understanding which are three parts of the *Spirit of God* (of which there appear to be seven). Moreover, in advanced cultures, the Serpent is often a half-human deity, with the serpent-female being the one who is important to humanity. In the case of the Scythians (original residents of modern Ukraine and Crimea) the serpent-female and half-mortal Hercules are credited with being the parents of Scythe, their founder and first king.

In the context of an All-wise and All-knowing deity, Eden's

Serpent would, like the Seven Angels of Revelation, be an agent of the Creator. If not for the fact that the Serpent retained its status as deity throughout the old and new world, the alleged punishment might be seen as a symbolic demotion. But reality seems to dictate it was simply the establishment of a second set of managerial agents – who would eventually replace, or oversee, Serpent activities.

Recognizing the ancient tradition of surrogates who will help move events along, we can look to The Tea Party Movement as the modern surrogates – their purpose being to gather in all who will be judged unfit and unworthy as the Book of Revelation prophecies unfold.

Appointing, or creating surrogates is not at all uncommon; if you are worthy of survival, they are easily identified.

First, there is no such thing as "original sin" – unless you are asserting a Creator who is imperfect, and too stupid to know that mandating an exclusive class of food, then creating the forbidden food as a desirable element in that mandated class – as opposed to any variety of possibilities that are forbidden – ensures violation of the prohibition. This is complicated by creating an entity who can communicate to humans, and a human entity which can reason.

Basically, the advocates of "original sin" are arguing their deity is an idiot. What parent would tell a child they can play with any ball they find, then tell them that one ball is off limits, and introduce someone into the house who KNEW (remember, they are all-knowing) would pickup the ball which should not be played with and then invite the child to play catch?

Of course, the events would make absolute sense, if the parent were using reverse psychology and wanted to justify being able to move the child into another realm of experience, but still be able to play the obedience card when necessary.

If we assume that eating the fruit was "original sin" and therefore a problem, than how much greater the sin of being told not to eat pork or shellfish – then celebrating divine holidays with the consumption of forbidden foods?

The Qur'an [3:7] truthfully and prophetically states:

"There are some who twist the Scripture with their tongues to make [people] think that what they say is part of the Scripture when it is not; they say it is from God when it is not; they attribute lies to God and they know it."

In Genesis, a primordial Creator, a self-begotten beginning, creates evolution – symbolically, or factually, the evolution of a being of clay or mud, a mindless Golem, into a thinking rational Homo Sapien Sapien. Man and woman are then raised above the prevailing archaic serpent deity – but with the recognition that there will always be a conflict between those who recognize the divinity of a rational self-begotten beginning, and those who insist upon tangible human icons and symbolically kowtow to serpents.

There is a lesson in the Qur'an which has been forgotten by those who do not care for their neighbor as they would themselves:

"No person to whom God had given the Scripture, wisdom, and prophesy would ever say to people, 'Be my servants, not God's.' ... He would never command you to take angels and prophets as lords. How could he command you to be disbelievers after you had devoted yourselves to God?" [3:79-80]

It is important to recognize that, in this context , the Qur'an is uses the term 'lords' as synonymous with "gods or saints". It is not diminishing the role of a prophet as a leader, king or president; in that capacity, Mohammad, Jesus, Moses, Aaron and Abraham were each depicted as both leaders and prophets – it doesn't matter to us if they were historic personages, or symbolic representations of the cultural leaders who introduced the tradition.

We cannot prove a Moses or Abraham, and some question the existence of a man who we call Jesus, but Mohammad appears to have been real, and DNA (the Cohen Modal Haplotype) indicates that there once was an Aaron (a Priest) who lived around 1300bce – and who is the direct common ancestor to those males who today claim Kohanim ancestry.

Religion is shaped by man and constitutes whatever man claims it to be – it is a means by which to understand existence. In the end, however, it comes down to the self-begotten beginning – the point in time when something emerged from nothing and the eternal nature of the universe.

There is no reason for the universe to be concerned with the particles contained within it, unless those particles are destructive to its very nature and existence. Prophecy might be seen as the means of warning a set of particles, or cells, that it has begun to turn destructive.

Prophecy is the universe responding to what it hears, sees, and experiences – even though we do not like to conceive of a deity needing to experience in the way that the ancient Greeks described the behavior of the Olympian beings. The universe could be viewed as a perfectly imperfect living organism.

The universe is, and must be, imperfect because perfection would mean perfect stability, and that would mean a lack of motion – all forces would balance and cancel each other out. Imperfection is achieved by parallel actions, obeying identical laws of sequential behavior in an unsynchronized manner which creates interactive random patterns. Those patterns allow for freewill – characteristic of all sentient being's.

A failure to comprehend the true nature of both freewill, and random action, explains the inability of some to understand both why "bad things happen to good people," and why all scriptures tell us we are responsible for our futures.

Prophecy is predicated on the assumption that all patterns of sequential behavior will continue, even though they are modified by their interaction with other patterns. In an ideal universe, these interactions will cause the patterns to coalesce toward an ideal state of imbalance – the religious concept of Heaven, or perfection in the absence of stagnation.

To fully understand the nature of prophecy, consider these words from Ecclesiastes 10:20:

> "Curse not the king, not even within thy thoughts; curse not the rich in thy bedchamber: for a bird of the air shall carry the voice, and make known that which has been said."

Snowden and Cruz
Surviving Prophecy

In 2013, an American computer specialist named Edward Joseph Snowden stepped into the history books – by revealing to the world that the National Security Agency (NSA) was engaged in the behavior depicted, or foretold, in Ecclesiastes 10:20.

Snowden is reported to have explained his revelations with the words, "I do not want to live in a world where everything I do and say is recorded... My sole motive is to inform the public as to that which is done in their name and that which is done against them."

But what did he actually revel? Other than the fact that very few people have every read, or understood, the words of Ecclesiastes 10:20 – or, in all probability, the words of their own parents.

Growing up as one of the last of the Silent Generation, which gave way to those who would be labeled a baby-boomer generation, my parents and grandparents impressed upon me the idea that you "do not air your dirty laundry in public"; never argue in public, or say anything that could be repeated – unless you want it repeated.

Hollywood, politicians and all who seek public limelight, are told to control their image. If you transmit information across airwaves, you have no means of controlling who sees it. In Hebrew speak: If you should watch your speech in the privacy of your own bedchamber, how much more so should you hold your tongue when outside?

The Snowden revelations about NSA have given meaning to the Hebrew expression *Oznayim la'kotel* ("the wall has ears"). The midrash warning which accompanies that expression states, "The wall has ears, the road has ears, and you cannot speak freely."

But why go back in time and assert ancient wisdom, when we need go no further back than the end of the Second World War and George Orwell's *"1984"*? Why should anyone be surprised that the government accesses information made freely available to any with the ears to hear, or eyes to see? Whatever is transmitted via public media is open to nondisruptive interception.

Personal privacy and Cyber security form the double edged sword of prophecy. Whatever will secure Instagrams and FaceBook chats will also give coverage to those who would conspire to destroy a nation.

It seems rather curious that, in the modern age, where each family – via there newest model car with all the electronic gizmos; or their home, with its internet access; or their cellphone, which is broadcasting their location – ... where each individual purchases the tools to make real the words "the wall and road have ears," it seems somewhat disingenuous to make an issue of those ears being used.

The ancient words become a prophecy of our age and the full extent to which words or actions can be spread. It is also a warning to heed the admonition against being a gossip or teller of tales and lies – we should consider teaching our children a few rather old words about how to behave when engaged in social networking:

A dishonest man spreads strife, and a whisperer separates close friends. [Proverbs 16:28]

Whoever goes about slandering reveals secrets; therefore do not associate with a simple babbler. [Proverbs 20:19]

Let no corrupting talk come out of your mouths, but only such as is good for building up, as fits the occasion, that it may give grace to those who hear. [Ephesians 4:29]

I tell you, on the day of judgment people will give account for every careless word they speak. [Matthew 12:36]

Given that we are in the final age of the Revelation Prophecy, the aforesaid words of Matthew take on serious meaning to any who believe in either the value of religion or Christian Prophecy.

Consider those admonitions in the context of the American political environment surrounding the 2014 midterm elections and the subsequent 2016 presidential battle.

The American Constitution requires that both a presidential and vice presidential candidate be "natural born citizens." Barack Obama was born in Honolulu, two years after Hawaiian statehood

– making him a 'natural born America'; Rafael Edward 'Ted' Cruz was born in Calgary, Alberta, Canada – rending him a 'natural born Canadian'. Those called Birthers attack Obama as ineligible to hold the Office of President, but find no inconsistency in supporting a Cruz candidacy for the office in 2016.

Cruz's father, Rafael Cruz Sr., is on record as asserting that Barack Obama was born in Kenya. In a sermon given at the New Beginnings Church in Irving, Texas, on August 26, 2012, Cruz Sr also called for "kings" such as his son Ted to rule America, and then take money from all non-evangelical Christians and redistribute it to fundamentalists – both clergy and parishioners.

At the same meeting, Pastor Larry Huch said, "I know that's why God got Rafael's son elected – Ted Cruz, the next Senator. But here's the exciting thing – and that's why I know it's timely for him to teach this, and bring this anointing. This will begin what we call the 'End Time Transfer of Wealth.' ... And that when these gentiles begin to receive this blessing, they will never go back financially through the valley again."

We thus know that he views this as the end-of-times spoken of in the *Book of Revelation*. Huch then went on to say, "God is looking at the church, and everyone in it, and deciding, in the next 3 and 1/2 years, who will be his bankers. And the ones that say, 'Here am I, Lord, you can trust me', we will become so blessed that we will usher in the coming of the Messiah."

Look at the 3.5 year, or 42 month, time period – consider it in terms of these two verses from *Revelation* and the extraordinary high profile afforded a freshman Senator:

But the Court which is without the Temple cast out, and mete it not, for it is given unto the Gentiles; and the holy city shall they tread under foot, two and forty months. [11:2]

And there was given unto him a mouth, that spake great things and blasphemies, and power was given unto him, to do two and forty months. [13:5]

When Washington is brought to its knees, as happened in the

2013 governmental Shutdown, might that be considered the same as treading the city under foot? And how might we view the 'bully pulpit' Cruz has been granted by the national Media?

In his sermon, Pastor Cruz asserted, "There are some of you, as a matter of fact I will dare to say the majority of you, that your anointing is not an anointing as priest. It's an anointing as king. And God has given you an anointing to go to the battlefield. And what's the battlefield? The battlefield is the marketplace. To go to the marketplace and occupy the land ... and take dominion."

Pastors Huch and Cruz have made their common position clear. Each jointly invoked the words of Revelation and prophecy to attest to their belief that we are in the 'End-of-Time" period and Ted Cruz is the anointed 'King', for it is said in *Matthew* that, at this in history, there will be:

Watch out for false prophets. They come to you in sheep's clothing, but inwardly they are ferocious wolves. [7:15]

For false Christs and false prophets will arise and will show great signs and wonders, so as to mislead, if possible, even the elect. Behold, I have told you in advance. [24:24-25]

Two pastors have invoked related words from Revelation, Matthew, Luke and John to describe Ted Cruz. We can attribute nothing of it, or attribute to it great significance – and justify both positions with the fact that they are pastors speaking 'in-bible' to a congregation.

Behind the pastors we find a second layer, a sectarian layer of wealth – the Koch brothers, who, in order to establish a clearly Republican control of the United States Senate, have spent tens of millions of dollars rebranding and then promoting false stories about the impact of a health care reform policy originally initiated by the Reagan-Bush-Bush Republican Administrations.

Are the Koch brothers playing the role spoken of in Exodus:

You shall not bear a false report; do not join your hand with a wicked man to be a malicious witness. [23:1]

Prophecy is fact and fiction. We can assert that the color of the sky reflects the electro-magnetic frequence of the gases which compose the atmosphere as it filters the rays of light; we can then assert the appearance of a naturally occurring color in association with some normally recurring event, and that becomes a prophecy. Obviously, coincidence will achieve the outcome – fulfillment – in the same way it could be fulfilled with meaning. The difference is the number of patterns which come together, combined with their causal relationship (the total context and their interrelationship to repeated events which occur within that context).

When people seek power through lies, they can often achieve the power, but only through war or generally experienced hardship.

Hitler could not have achieved power if the experience of war had not altered his personality, and if Germany were not already anti-Semitic. But, since anti-Semitism is a common element in the prophecies, it follows that it has to be present as a unifier of hatred or to serve as an external focus of social unrest.

Throughout 2013 and into 2014, the media was speaking of governmental, legislative, attacks on circumcision and kosher slaughter – not traditional anti-Semitism, because the focus of the attacks is the discomfort caused by Islamic terrorism, and Islam follows the Semitic-Israelite laws.

In March 2014, the Kremlin has issued more condemnations of anti-Semitism than in the preceding decade; anti-Semitism was on the lips of the Russian Ambassador to the United Nations, their Foreign Minister, and even President Vladimir Putin.

Their focus was on non-Russian anti-Semites and Ukrainian "Neo-Nazism, fascism and anti-Semitism" as a justification for a continued and increased presence of Russian troops in the Crimea.

Following the official lead, journalist Alexander Prokhanov warned: "I'm especially astonished by the Jewish organizations that support this Maidan. Don't they understand that they are helping bring on a second Holocaust?"

The historic sponsor of pogroms is now playing its Jewish card to justify a possible expansion of activities beyond a Crimean boundary and on to the historically disputed Galician territories. At home, the Russian Parliament passed a law allowing it to quickly block any undesirable website and thereby expand their traditional control over media and communications. The roads and walls both have ears – do not aid the unintended listener.

If we think of the related prophecies, the use of 'the elect' and 'the Chosen' to reference the Hebrews and distinguish them from those who face the greatest hardships, we have a completely different version of events than that portrayed by the; those who say the are Jews but are not."

When we speak of prophecy, we speak of a variation on the words of George Santayana: "Those who cannot remember the past are condemned to repeat it." The past is not always an action, it is also an ability to observe the nature of problems. Prophets derive their skill from an assumption that the average person will always be ignorant of history; ignorance allows those who know history to utilize past persuasion techniques to shape their rise to power – but knowledge also allows the wise to warn of the patterns associated with the unscrupulous advancement of evil.

Roads and walls have ears. Three thousand years ago that was a metaphor designed to ensure one would be politically correct – even in the confines of their own bedchamber, where the lesson of Sampson and Delia was always a potential reality. But today it is a reality. We carry the ears with us; we purchase and install them in our homes; we have them control our homes and happily obtain apps which will allow us, or any who hack our systems, to open and close doors, windows, even control the faucets on our kitchen sinks.

We work to fulfill prophecy, to disregard ancient warnings, to become the people we were warned against. And now we are at a point in history where those people are manipulating us.

In Matthew 24, we were warned that two people could be sanding together, and one would die while the other lived. The Book of Revelation modified that warning – making it one in three.

The warnings go unheeded. One such warning – one most ignored by those who claim to believe – is that we should judge people by their deeds and not their words. What are the deeds of those who claim to be 'fiscally responsible' Conservatives?

The Dates
Events of our age

	Metonic						
	51		**52**			**53**	
	HY	CE	HY	CE	millennial	HY	CE
Jesus Birth	3755	(7)	3755	(7)	3755	(7)	3755	(7)
Era 1	4724	962	4743	981	4755	993	4762	1000	Rev
White Horseman	5693	1931	5731	1969	5755	1993	5769	2007	6:02

2 Therefore I beheld, and lo, there was a white horse, and he that sat on him, had a bow, and a crown was given unto him, and he went forth conquering that he might overcome.

Jesus Calendar	3762	1	3762	1	3762	1	3762	1
Era 1	4731	970	4750	989	4762	1001	4769	1008	Rev
Red Horseman	5700	1939	5738	1977	5762	2001	5776	2015	6:04

4 And there went out another horse, that was red, and power was given to him that sat thereon to take peace from the earth, and that they should kill one another, and there was given unto him a great sword.

Crucified	3794	33	3794	33	3794	33	3794	33
Era 1	4763	1002	4782	1021	4794	1033	4801	1040	Rev
Black Horseman	5732	1971	5770	2009	5794	2033	5808	2047	6:05

5 And when he had opened the third seal, I heard the third beast say, Come and see. Then I beheld, and lo, a black horse, and he that sat on him, had balances in his hand.

6 And I heard a voice in the midst of the four beasts say, A measure of wheat for a penny, and three measures of barley for a penny, and oil, and wine hurt thou not.

Temple Destroyed	3830	69	3830	69	3830	69	3830	69
Era 1	4799	1038	4818	1057	4830	1069	4837	1076	Rev
Pale Horseman [Death]	5768	2007	5806	2045	5830	2069	5844	2083	6:08

Hades (Hell) Followed	Rev
	6:08

8 And I looked, and behold, a pale horse, and his name that sat on him was Death, and Hell followed after him, and power was given unto them over the fourth part of the earth, to kill with sword, and with hunger, and with death, and with the beasts of the earth.

With Four Horsemen there are four possible date sequences, which we will examine in the next chapter. For now we can assert, if you believe in prophecy, regardless of the sequence, the world has entered the final era in the Revelation Prophecies – which infers we are in the Era of all biblical prophecy.

Both Christianity and Islam are fundamentally predicated on the existence of prophecy, and have a vested interest in its accuracy being clearly established.

However, Judaism is not predicated on prophecy, or that which might happen in the future. Rather its basis is the covenant, divine promise, and absolute assurance that adherence to medical, dietary, and hygienic Laws will ensure Jewish survival against all who seek its destruction.

For Jews, prophecy is an indication of the events which will befall the Gentiles, events which the Hebrews must prepare for in the same way that Noah was told to prepare for the Flood brought about by the mythical Deluge.

While the Deluge was mythical, the Flood was symbolic of the realities of life on this planet. Those who are forewarned, and do not scoff, will – like the animals over which they have dominion – survive. Those who scoff at reality will become extinct.

The prophecies which were eventually combined to generate the Book of Revelation are speaking to the realities of our age. They tell us that they are projected two thousand years into the future – they even place emphasis on things we must focus upon if we wish to fulfill the role of Noah and escape the inevitable calamity.

Look at the illustration, the verse [6:6] encased in the grey box.

The American State Department underestimated the amount of greenhouse gas emissions associated with development of the proposed Keystone XL pipeline and downplays the significance the pipeline would have for development of the Canadian tar sands.

The purpose of the pipeline project, is to connect Alberta's tar sands oil to Gulf refineries. But reality demands we question why it isn't cheaper to build a new refinery – one which does not require the piping of poisonous crude oil through farmlands.

Because State Department's report failed to fully consider the ways the pipeline would affect production of the tar sands, they deemed insignificant pipeline within the broader context of either the rate of oil sand extraction, or the demand for heavy crude oil at refineries in the United States. One key point which was ignored is that the price of oil would have to be higher to make shipping by rail, as opposed to pipeline, cost effective. Lower transportation costs mean higher production for the same cost-profit model.

In the context of international climate negotiations, the U.S. established as a goal the cutting of emissions by 17 percent below 2005 levels by 2020. But the offsetting equation indicates that Keystone makes that goal impossible, this mandates an inevitable failure to meeting stated climate goals, and undermines the concept of a climate-safe world. However, it does ensure a world according to the Book of Revelation prophecy and the depiction of America as the referenced Babylon.

If we recall the prophecy, we remember it warned of water being polluted, which is exactly what the Keystone XL pipeline project threatens to the huge Ogallala aquifer which supports the Nebraska and Kansas farming industry. Collapse that industry and we have the words of verse 6:8 – which proclaims the cost of wheat and barley in a context of protecting oil before a Fourth Horseman appears.

Climate scientist James Hansen looked at the pipeline in terms of the effect fossil fuels have on climate change, and said, "the fuse to the biggest carbon bomb on the planet." Obviously, those who are working to destroy the planet – who represent the seven vials of wrath which are to be spilled on the earth and into the water [15:7; 16:2; 16:4] – would promote something which is properly described a pipeline over the Ogallala aquifer as one of the biggest energy, or environmental, risks this America could currently take.

If we focus on the Canadian shale oil, the same threat to water is emerging from the Enbridge Line 9 pipeline — from North Westover, Ontario, to Montreal – which is aimed at a link to South

Portland, Maine. To achieve the connection, the pipeline would bring toxic tar sands oil to New England, where it will flow south through Vermont, New Hampshire and Maine.

As Senator Angus King pointed out, "... this pipeline runs through very important — and ecologically fragile — parts of Maine, including Sebago Lake, the drinking water supply for the greater Portland area."

If a tar sands pipeline were to spill into the Sebago-Crooked River watershed the result would be devastating to the Sebago-Crooked River watershed lake, its fisheries and southern Maine's clean drinking water supply. All of which would fulfill the purpose of the vial which the third Angel poured into "rivers and fountains of waters," [16:4] so they would be contaminated.

The scales are in play, the hearts (or souls) of men are to be weighed – as the ancient Egyptians might have said, "against the weight of a feather."

Given a potential for destruction of the watertable in two areas of the nation, consider this: In the United States, California produces roughly half the fruit and vegetables grown and therefore the water required to produce water intensive foods like walnuts, broccoli, lettuce, tomatoes, strawberries, almonds and grapes is a significant point of focus.

California uses 80 percent of its water for agriculture, if there was a poisoning of the northwest aquifer, that could cause their water dependency to create cascading stress on those resources needed by California; add a drought and half the shelves in produce sections of stores across the nation would be empty. And that would be before a discussion of the loss of animal feed and poultry, beef, and pork production – with related financial collapses in the farm related sectors of the nation.

The 2007-2008 financial collapse was contributed to by banks having an incentive to grant mortgages to high risk borrowers – the effect was to drive home prices upward through the associated increased demand. The banks reduced, or eliminated, their risks by bundling their mortgages into bonds secured and supported by the mortgage payments – thus default only occurred when homeowners stopped making their monthly payments.

By overloading the bonds with high risk lenders, and retaining the low risk ones as part of the bank portfolio, any waver in the economy could cause a collapse in real estate related bond markets.

The demographics of the real estate market created a second dynamic: as populations age, or decline, the demand for housing shrinks. Zero population growth, combined with the aging baby-boomer generation, mandates a glut of housing originally built to accommodate baby-boomer demand.

Unfortunately, the economic models used to measure the American economy utilize "housing starts" as a key number; this reflects 1950's economic theory models which are no longer valid – and are made less valid by the anti-immigration policies imposed by the Republican wing of the Federal Government. Simply put, zero population growth, accompanied by total household equilibrium, is required to sustain all models based on 1950's economic theories.

Those economic models are also connected to anti-socialist psychologies which denounce single-payer government policies.

The Tea Party Republican battle against the Affordable Care Act is a continuation of the discredited thinking which promotes those outdated policies.

The record shows that the assertions against what has been dubbed Obamacare have proved false and unsubstantiated by any factual arguments.

Comically, the Qur'an [3:118] warns people of these people: "You who believe, do not take for your intimates such outsiders as spare no effort to ruin you and want to see you suffer: their hatred is evident from their mouths, but what their hearts conceal is far worse."

In addition to their attack on Obamacare, 208 Republicans co-sponsored the *Save American Workers Act of 2013*, introduced by Republican Representative Todd Young of Indiana. The intent of that legislation was to modify the definition of a full-time worker from 30 hours per week to 40 hours of steady employment. The goal was to circumvent the employer mandate in the Affordable Care Act.

The argument was that 40-hours is the historical norm, and maintaining it protects working poor and middle class employees by providing a definition which is legally consistent with other laws governing employment. Had this definitional modification to the law passed, the immediate effect would have been two-fold: first it wound have achieved the goal of disqualifying various firms from providing coverage under ACA; second it would have disqualified one million workers from insurance coverage they already received under pre-existing insurance policies. In short, the objective was to disenfranchise millions of Americans from their existing coverage.

In terms of the Federal budget, half of those disenfranchise workers would be forced into an alternative – non-employer based – ACA plan, or would become qualified under Medicaid. Those who are left wouldn't have any health insurance at all.

Naturally, Medicaid qualification via welfare would drive up the deficit. That increase would be compounded by the proposed "employee protection" which would loosen employer penalty for non-compliance under ACA and thereby increase the deficit by $74 billion.

Since a 40-hour work week would have been the criteria, employers would be free to drop employee hours to 35 – possibly by redefining their "lunch-hour" and "coffee-break" provisions, and adjusting pay upward to reflect hours "actually worked exclusive of scheduled breaks." Thus allowing the employee to receive the same pay for 35-hours they were receiving for 40. There would be pay ramifications for overtime, but these would be compensated for by other offsetting savings tied to the use of 40-hours in contracts and related laws which the "employee protection act" was supposedly being consistent with – with a net loss to the employees.

One very obvious aspect of "employee protection" is a clear refusal to increase the minimum wage.

In preparation for America's 2014 mid-term elections, the

Republicans, along with Democrats up for reelection in districts where there is the perception of a strong Tea Party Movement, are opposing a minimum wage increase from $7.25 to $10.10 an hour in time for the 2016 presidential election.

The argument against a wage increase is the possibility that, over the next three year, it might reduce employment by 500,000 workers. However, that does not take into account the benefits of a higher minimum wage for tens of millions of workers and the broader economy. When that is figured in, America would gain a higher pay base (foundation), lower poverty, less turnover and more spending – the result being increased employment to meet retail service demands.

Republicans concerns over job loss are negated by their disregard for, and opposition to, reinstatement of federal jobless benefits which expired in 2014 – with a net loss to the American economy of over 200,000 jobs. That job loss being a direct effect of the decreased purchasing power represented by the withheld funds.

The Republicans have also promoted federal food stamps cuts which will be costing another 75,000 jobs by the end of 2014 – with no economic benefits.

There is a consistency of pattern: in each instance, without exception, the rules keep changing – with one goal in mind – ensure the most harm to the most people. To achieve that objective, poor people must be kept poor and, ideally, sick; the rich should receive services without having to pay for them – providing they support the policy of harm.

Winning become so important to the Tea Party that its vocal elements believe they need to win at all costs. Their sense of self-worth is so fragile that they can't endure the idea of losing to those who are socially and economically rational. Moreover, they play to the irrational elements of American society. That specific social element is incapable of conceptionalizing the disconnect between claims of fiscal responsibility and runaway national debt which is accompanied by a decrease in their quality of life – as represented by a decline in the purchasing power of a dollar and minimum wage living standards.

Look at the tantrums thrown by those Tea Party Republican candidates in 2014 and 2016 – as initiated by the one thrown in 2013, when they closed down the government and held the lawful debt obligations of the United States for ransom. That little temper tantrum threatened the stability of the global economy, which is the prediction associated with the fall of "Babylon the Great City."

Grow and victory does not come solely from winning, we can grow more from losing – if we do it properly. In a proper victory, as in a proper loss, both opponents rise to the next level of existence and prosper together. When the result of deceit is adoption of a lie, victory cannot be attained.

Think about Saint Paul's Joke – forty percent of the Christian scriptures are predicated on the idea that the true Gentile will never understand it; therefore will become victims of Revelation – they are among the third who shall die, who must die. Why must they die? Because it is clearly an objective of those promoting The Tea Party Movement.

Let's examine the truth or falsely of assertions made by the Tea Party Republicans about The Affordable Care Act (Obamacare).

First of all, as pointed out in the media and the book, "*The Tea Party: America Upended*", the healthcare imitative originated as a Conservative Republican private sector program. The purpose was to meet the growing economic need for affordable medica care in the context of a capitalist system – as opposed to the single payer National Health Care systems being adopted by capitalist nations who were outperforming America.

There was a realization that National Health Care systems were more effective than tariffs, quotas, or other restrictive trade programs designed to produce a competitive advantage to products involved in international commerce. National Health Care systems are purely internal and therefore are not subject to international trade agreements of laws, but, by removing the cost concerns over health, and ensuring that their workers are healthy, they do affect both the productivity and purchasing power of workers.

Propelling Prophecy
Agents for dating abound.

There is a harsh reality to an environment in which prophecy and prediction have little meaning: We lack historical perspective and the willingness to grand the time necessary for any reasonable qualitative analysis. We 'knowing' the facts, because we have heard them, or seen them via our Wi-Fi connection. Few people care to know the actual source of that information, devote time to consider any implications their triggered response might have for themselves or their families.

A Ted Cruz can stand on the floor of the Senate and declare that the Affordable Care Act (re-branded as Obamacare and thereby granting Obama the full benefits of any legacy which might emerge) is bad, it is a disaster, it cannot possibly work.

But, given the opportunity to speak, Ted Cruz chose to read Dr Seuss rather than explain why it is wrong to provide the poorest workers with privatized medical coverage. Why is it wrong to have the private sector extend coverage to workers who previously could not afford it, or who afford it, but were denied coverage because of a 'pre-existing medical condition'? Why is it preferable to allow the insurers to impose gender based discrimination in premiums they charge to employers?

We hear of increased costs – some attributed to increased coverage, or benefits, and others due to increased co-payments and deductibles. Problem with most of those alleged increased costs? They fail to reflect the income based government subsidies, and are generally complained about by those who have been underpaying for their coverage – those who were ripping off the system – or who, if they were to get sick, would rather be stuck with the full cost for their treatment, rather than 20-percent of that cost. Why the full cost? Because their previous policies didn't cover the things which are most likely to befall them.

For decades insurers employed low level clerks to overrule the recommendation of doctors, or to find an excuse to avoid paying for those treatments. In many cases, insurers had been collecting premiums for policies against which there were never claims, but when a claim is filed, they find an excuse not to honor their portion of the contract. That is dishonest – but it is a dishonesty which The Tea Party Movement fully supports and effectively advocates for.

While rational people can argue the projections of real and imagined effects, the ultimate question is one of: Why would any political party seek to deny a sixth part of its constituents medical care – especially when it is a privatized Capitalist system which will actually be footing the cost and reaping the benefits.

Prophecy tells us that their will be agents of evil who will seek to harm as many people as possible. Those agents will seek to bring as many people as possible into their camp, and the result will be a third to half of the overall population being judged unfit.

Deceit and dishonesty characterize the primary agents for the fulfillment of end-of-times prophecy. The Four Horsemen of the Apocalypse represent the characteristics of the years in which those agents will make their appearances. Because those dates and cycles were considered in terms of the Hebrew Calendar, when we convert to our modern calendar there is a two year 'lead-in period' (plus or minus one year from the first day of the New Year in the Hebrew Calendar) to the years presented in the 'Events of our age' Chart.

We have a range date chart – the upper date represents the probable intended date; below it is the lower end event start date. The Metonic cycles [51, 52, 53] represent those associated with the number of 19-year periods in Methuselah's age; those for the year Enoch died; those that would span a millennial period (1007 years).

	Metonic								
	51		52			53			
	HY	CE	HY	CE	millennial	HY	CE		
White Horseman	5693	1931 / 1929	5731	1969 / 1967	5755 / 1993 / 1991	5769	2008 / 2006		6:02
Red Horseman	5700	1939 / 1937	5738	1977 / 1975	5762 / 2001 / 1999	5776	2015 / 2013		6:04
Black Horseman	5732	1971 / 1969	5770	2009 / 2007	5794 / 2033 / 2031	5808	2047 / 2045		6:05
Pale Horseman [Death]	5768	2007 / 2005	5806	2045 / 2043	5830 / 2069 / 2067	5844	2083 / 2081		6:08
Hades (Hell) Followed									6:08

We first see that the White Horseman emerges in the period between 1929-1931, the precise years associated with Hitler's Nazi Party. Is it really necessary to expound on his influence, or forces at work when the Red Horseman appears between 1937 and 1939?

The White *"went forth conquering that he might overcome"*; the Red receive the power *"to take peace from the earth, and that they should kill one another, and there was given unto him a great sword."* Could anyone deny these events describe the Axis Powers in World War Two?

The White and Black Horsemen came together in 1969 – when the Black Horseman, who "had balances in his hand," and America was undergoing the turmoil associated with opposition to the Vietnam Conflict. It was a year in which Richard Nixon was elected President – bringing with him a vice-President who would be booted from office and justice would see the President resign in disgrace. The Black Horseman's Scales of Justice had their effect on history.

The White Horsemen spans the year 2007, which is shared by both the Black and Pale Horsemen and marks a Global Recession which attacked – and possibly corrected – inequities of economies, and, in prophecy, was preceded by voices declaring, *"A measure of wheat for a penny, and three measures of barley for a penny, and oil, and wine hurt thou not."*

The Pale Horseman is Death – and he is followed by Hades – and *"power was given unto them over the fourth part of the earth, to kill with sword, and with hunger, and with death, and with the beasts of the earth."* We need only read the news reports to see if this holds relevance to the world we know.

I chose to lessen the importance of the Red Horseman in 2001 – painting it grey. We know of the 9/11 attack and the false claims by President George W. Bush about WMD's (Weapons of Mass Destruction) in Iraq which were used to justify the murder of Saddam Hussein and destabilization of that nation.

The emphasized year, 1999, is the year Nostradamus stated the Great King of Terror would appear, and that would seem to be enough to explain the 9/11 events and a dozen years of killing which the United States subsequently sponsored and financed.

This brings us to the final years for the Red Horseman, 2013 through 2015 – the years in which The Tea Party attacked both its own parent Republican Party, and President Barack Obama. This is the period in which the Right to Life – the right to live a healthy and productive life – was attacked on the floor of the United States Senate.

In terms of Religion, and the lessons in *"Saint Paul's Joke,"* 2013 marked the resignation of Pope Benedict XVI and installation of Francis I as [possibly] the 112th and final Pope in the eleventh century papal list prophecy by St. Malachy. That prophecy has the 112th legitimate Pope witnessing the destruction of the Vatican and Rome.

In Revelation this is reported as the destruction of the City of the Seven Hills and the Church of Satan; if these are the same location, than the prophecies describe Roman Christianity, and its Protestant or Evangelical offspring, as Satanic. [17:9]

Though, in fairness, Wikipedia lists cities which claim to be constructed on seven hills – and there are quite a few. The problem is isolating one (other than Rome) which can clearly be associated with a significant Church – one that can be called "the whore of Babylon." If The united States is Babylon, and represents itself to be a 'Christian Nation,' than the Whore might be the Evangelicals, or the native Mormon Church.

And 2013 was marked by the American Government being Shutdown, and The Tea Party Republicans unanimously declaring their willingness to destroy the Global Economy rather than allow the poorest workers the right to buy affordable healthcare coverage.

The Horsemen continue to ride, with Black and Pale coming together in the year 2045, to celebrate the centennial of the first use of Atomic Bombs in war, or death of the Baby-Boom generation?

Will 2045 be a year in which the bomb, once again, is used to achieve some purpose – albeit allegedly expressing Divine Wrath, or will it simply mark a change in global economics?

Seven ... Really?
What's with the numbers

Would you buy a phone number – especially they might only allow you to keep it for two years?

Would you pay 2.1 million dollars (7,877,777 dirhams) for a two year 'lucky number' phone contract? Especially if you then had to pay an additional $230 per month to maintain it?

That is exactly what the winning bidder at a charity auction in Abu Dhabi did, and paid, for number 777-7777 – seven-sevens.

To be the seventh son of a seventh son is, as readers of the Arabian Nights know, a very auspicious status.

In Hebrew, seven-sevens represents a unit of dry measure, and, as mentioned in *"OMER* the Patriarch 49," a unit of measure which, in the Hebrew Calendar of holidays, in terms of days, it is the period between the Jewish holidays of Passover and Shavuot, and in years is immediately followed by the Jubilee Year of Release – an end of seven cycles of *shmita* (Sabbatical years) and time when property rights are restored:

"This fiftieth year is sacred—it is a time of freedom and of celebration when everyone will receive back their original property, and slaves will return home to their families." [Leviticus 25:10]

It is taught that, in the fiftieth year, oppression is forbidden; it is also said that the Jubilee marks a special year for the remission of sins and the granting of forgiveness.

But there is a mysticism which seems to track the Sabbatical years, and therefore the Jubilee.

If, using the Hebrew dates in *"Genesis of Genesis,"* we count Jubilee years from the Exodus in HY2455, we can look to our year 2026 (HY5777) – specifically Saturday, 12 September – as the next critical point in the sequence, with the Red Horseman year HY5738 (1977) as the last year of comparable significance.

Was there any Red Horseman significance in the year that

Jimmy Carter was inaugurated? Or should we be looking back two years, to the lower end of the spread, and the Fall of Saigon?

Or maybe the Red Horseman's role of taking peace should be focused on a symbolic 'Great Sword' – the creation of Microsoft and Apple Computer, which would eventually give birth to the internet and implementation of the technologies which would give both the walls and roads their ears?

The structure of the prophecies in Revelation follow a pattern of sevens. The pattern of sevens is so coincidental. Count back two sevens from 2026 and you have 2012 – the year in which Ted Cruz was elected to the Senate.

Could we envision a Tea Party Movement without its most visual and outspoken member?

Should we dismiss everything as coincidence?

A rabbi once told the story of a man desperately looking for parking in midtown Manhattan. After the routinely interminable cycle of circling his block and hoping, he turned his eyes toward the sky and inwardly promises, "Lord, if you help me find a spot, I will donate ten percent of my firm's profit to charity."

Having no sooner had he finished the thought, but he caught sight of a neighbor getting into their car. Looking up, he said "It's okay, forget it, I found one."

Coincidences can be interesting.

If not for coincidence, we would be assured of certainty.

Should rational people care about mystical pronouncements of vaguely identified ancient prophets? Should we really devote this much time trying to understand or apply the means by which some symbol, or metaphor, could reflect a reality of our times? Especially if that reality is independent of the words and could be coincidence.

Does it make sense for someone – regardless of how much money they have to squander, or divert from the assistance of their fellow humans – to spend $2.1 million for a 'lucky phone number?'

Does that make more, or less, sense than the actions of some politicians attacking programs intended to help others?

Where are the facts to support the attacks? Where are the figurative WMD's behind the Affordable Care Act?

Where are the death panels?

In 2013, the media reported Time Magazine's senior political analyst Mark Halperin's statement that: "The Affordable Care Act contains provisions for "death panels," which decide which critically ill patients receive care and which don't. It's built into the plan. It's not like a guess or like a judgment. That's going to be part of how costs are controlled."

Certainly if death panels existed the evidence would be easily produced – after all, allegedly "It's built into the plan." Could he have been referring to the routine practice of private insurers to deny payment of claims? Is that what was meant by assertions the associated Medical care would be rationed? Are they asserting the private sector is that dishonest and untrustworthy – if so, they are arguing for a reliable National Health Service.

Does the law doesn't cut Medicare benefits, or hurt them in any way? Does it add to the deficit, or reduce it by $109 billion over ten years?

Is it a single payer socialized government takeover, or is it an expansion of an established private sector product? If it is not from the private sector, why are traditional insurers issuing the policies?

Is it, as some have claimed, unconstitutional? If so, where is the court challenge?

The program was created by traditional Reagan Republicans – beginning with Ronald Reagan himself. It's the antithesis of what has been called socialized medicine – in many ways that makes it the antithesis of Christian teachings and doctrine which mandates both 'Good Samaritan' behavior and rendering to Caesar that which is Caesar's. The latter mandating that you honor any secular, or governmental, law not inherently or clearly definitively immoral.

The rules of economics being what they are, Obamacare will – like an above poverty minimum wage ACA – cause a restructuring of the economy which will bring it into the twenty-first century and result in the creation millions of jobs. But Luddite mentality is the mentality of stagnation and traditional familiarity; it is far easier to sell the idea of never improving, than it is to convince people they will be better off tomorrow.

If you neither have children, nor envision yourself living to any point where tomorrow is a meaningful concept, than you can afford to be a Luddite. If you don't care about your neighbor any more than you care about yourself, being a Luddite is the ideal.

The Tea Party speaks to Luddites. It says everything is bad, and offers nothing to address the problems which are indisputably bad. But that does not stop things from changing.

Over the past 50 years – a single Jubilee cycle – international commerce has caused diets around the world to change, to congeal into a 'globalized' menu which has cost us diversity and made the world dependant upon a few key crops, and thereby rendered us all susceptible to the failure of a few crops.

As previously mentioned, California produces roughly half the fruit and vegetables grown in the United States. America is a major agricultural exporter – has been since the 1960's – therefore a crop failure there would impact populations in diverse nations.

On the other hand, America imports many common foods, and every advanced nation must ask: "To what degree are common foods imported?" Cultivated crop diversity has declined by 75% in the past century; a third of today's diversity will disappear by 2050.

On multiple levels, *Revelation* tells us that a third will vanish. We need no 'Divine Intervention' or 'Wrath' – by 2050, a third of the population (the Baby-boomers) will be gone from a world we know is experiencing negative reproductive growth; a third of crop diversity; consider the proportion of land covered by water from the melting glaciers; the percentage of potable water polluted by human commercial activities which are technologically antiquated – a third of each '*vial*' might prove a reasonable estimate.

As an homogenization of diet expedites non-communicable diseases associated with genetic adaptation to local diet, we see the prevalence of obesity, heart disease and diabetes increasing. This is an ideal justification for opposing healthcare legislation.

Luddite 2014
Looking to 2033

The Black Horseman carries scales of justice, or commerce, into the years 2031 to 2033 – according to the millennial scale from the probable year of crucifiction. Without exact dates there is no basis to extrapolate the dates for predicted events. The idea that you will not know the exact day and hour is concealed in the factual knowledge that you have been denied the starting point – so cannot know where to end the measured miles. But you do know that two thousand is two thousand and the period lay ahead of the speaker.

The calculation used in "Saint Paul's Joke," and the one by Sir Isaac Newton three centuries earlier, both yielded a period which began in 2034 and ended in roughly thirty years later.

On Thursday, 14 March 2014, Bill Gates told an audience at the American Enterprise Institute that we were twenty years away from an era of "software substitution" that will dramatically reduce the demand for many types of jobs.

Gates was speaking about the next Industrial Revolution. He was looking down the road and seeing – as a reality – what has been a part of science fiction for over a century. In 2027, a century will have passed since the world was exposed to the *Maschinenmensch* – the Machine-Human we now call Robots, Cyborgs, or, in the bible based sci-fi series *Battlestar Galactica*, Cylons – through the silent movie *Metropolis*.

Think about the meaning behind "software substitution", if we look to the centennial of that influential movie, thirteen years after the 2014 mid-term elections many of the concepts could be daily reality.

Think about it.

"Software substitution" means software automation, like the computer, "Hal" in Stanley Kubrick's 1968 film, *2001 A Space Odyssey* – the next generation of intelligent machines.

A century ago, who would have imagined that people on the

opposite side of the globe would have been able to clip something to their ears and speak as they strolled down their respective streets.

Today we have the possibility of looking at a single election cycle and later realizing it determined the course of history for the United States.

Just as the original Industrial Revolution could be seen to have changed the meaning of "menial jobs," the new Industrial Revolution will create a situation where many of the jobs that would be eliminated are lower skill occupations – making education more important.

Gates equated "Software substitution" changes to those low skill occupations which are already beginning to vanish – think about the rows of telephone switchboard operators who once were a defining element of telephone exchanges prior to the era of the direct dial circuits. Then came the era of secretarial switchboard operators who would direct you call within a company. Think about how different our telephone systems are today.

Gates predicted: "Technology over time will reduce demand for jobs, particularly at the lower end of skill set." As with telephone networks, each advance will substantially lower labor demand for what are now common skill sets. Yet our political system retains its Luddite mentality, and promotes that mentality among those who will be the most affected by our changing world of technology.

For Gates, part of the answer was to update, or alter, the tax codes to provide an economic stimulus to encourage companies to hire employees. He even went so far as to suggest we do away with income and payroll taxes entirely.

Of course that would mean the tax codes would need to compensate by eliminating tax deductions for business and significantly increasing the tax burden imposed upon domestic corporations – which would provide an economic incentive for more companies to outsource, or relocate, to other countries, with the effect of eliminating all meaningful domestic employment and creating an environment in which "Software substitution" would account for all the remaining jobs.

Having failed to follow his own logic to its conclusion, Gates also warned against raising the national minimum wage out of fear that it will prevent employers from hiring new workers. But the minimum wage is the wage paid to the very workers whose jobs are doomed by the inevitable approaching impacted of future "software substitution" – a fact which Gates actually argued, but did not seem to grasp.

Those who subscribe to ideal of The Tea Party Movement are in the same position demonstrated by Bill Gates – they are arguing a position without grasping its reality and ultimate consequences.

The fulfillment of prophecy relies upon the understanding that people do not grasp the ultimate consequences of their actions. Moreover, if we think in terms of Gates and Microsoft, "software substitution" is Microsoft's business; therefore Gates' business is to displace, or facilitate the displacement of, low skill workers.

Recognizing that, if minimum wages were to be raised now, there would be an incentive for companies to seek out "substitution software" – thus creating the appropriate market incentives for the non-Microsoft related development of related software packages.

In a business context, keeping the minimum wage low gives Microsoft time to identify specific low skill occupations which lend themselves to near-term "software substitution." The firm could then develop and beta test, software packages or applications which could be used to displace those workers.

Let's apply this type of *sub rosa* thinking to the actions which The Tea Party Movement demonstrated in 2013 and into 2014.

The attacks on Obamacare began with the rebranding of the Affordable Care Act into a healthcare initiative devoid of any clear connection with the Republican Party and an established history of Conservative Republican failures to pass the same privatize health expansion program.

Having rebranded privatized health care they proceeded to do everything within their power to deny the sick access to the new expanded program. In Maine, Republican Governor Paul LePage went to far as to declare Medicaid expansion for the poor "Sinful."

Typical of the national objection is that demonstrated by the Maine Republican Party – which seeks to deny coverage to 70,000 low-income Maine residents.

In Maine, in 2013, the Republicans raised certain objections to ACA related legislation; in 2014, The Maine Senate voted on a bill which recognized and addressed all the Republican objections – to ensure the sick would be denied care, they voted against their own recommendations. It has become self-evident that Republicans are so committed to their own empty rhetoric and loathing of ACA that they can't even accept legislation that recognized their demands.

The refusal to win is symbolic of an entity which is intent on stopping the game, or, at the very least, forcing it into overtime. In the context of biblical prophecy, when the game is over, Satan gets put down; so Satan has every reason to delay the final score.

LePage justifies denial of benefits on the grounds of personal experience: he worked his way out of poverty, so everyone else can do the same – no governmental assistance required or provided.

If we look at the arguments put forth by Tea Party supporter, we find they don not believe they should pay for anyone else – at the same time they promote tax 'loopholes' designed to see to it that they do not even pay for the services they receive: that everyone else pays for benefits Tea Party supporter receive from being American.

Supposedly, health insurance is a "disincentive to work," yet Norway, which provides all its citizens free healthcare, has greater economic output per hour worked than the United States.

In February 2014, The Congressional Budget Office reported ACA will boost demand for goods and services and, in turn, labor to provide them. The same can be said for increasing the minimum wage, and changing the overtime pay regulations – both of which will provide disposable income and therefore increase demand for goods and services.

But the Luddites hate progress and promote hardship.

In the decades ahead, but population and (what are now) low level jobs will vanish, but the need for healthy, productive workers – with better educations – will only grow.

Election 2016
A Lull Before The Storm

Politicians can use empty rhetoric to argue the various aspects of The Affordable Care Act, and whether the Obamacare Medicaid expansion should be implemented in Tea Party controlled states, but ultimately a decision should be based on the simple fact that health care improves people's quality of life – and Life, along with Liberty and the Pursuit of Happiness were unalienable rights asserted in the United States Declaration of Independence.

In the rough draft, Thomas Jefferson wrote:

We hold these truths to be sacred & undeniable; that all men are created equal & independent, that from that equal creation they derive rights inherent & inalienable, among which are the preservation of life, & liberty, & the pursuit of happiness ...

In the final edit, this then became the familiar:

We hold these truths to be self-evident, that all men are created equal, that they are endowed by their Creator with certain unalienable Rights, that among these are Life, Liberty and the pursuit of Happiness ...

One must wonder if the sick enjoy the same quality of life as the healthy, and whether the *Good Samaritan* parable was – as Tea Party supporters seem to assert – a cautionary tale about someone who should be allowed to fend for himself, and the Samaritan who was wrong to abandon the pattern associated with his people.

Clearly the Republican Tea Party interpretation is that only those who can pay are entitled to access to lifesaving medicines or preventive care. The merchant-victim in the parable lost his right to care the minute his attackers left with his money – at least that is the position of Tea Party Movement members.

The grey Enoch date for the Black Horseman is 2009, the following year the Tea Party presented its official presence on the political scene – on 14 March it launched its initial protest against the Patient Protection and Affordable Care Act; thus they formally declaring their disdain and outright hatred for all those who are cursed with poor health, or, like the victim in the Good Samaritan parable, the need for emergency medical attention.

We need to remember that each of the Horsemen represents some aspect of divine wrath, and the Black Horseman carries scales which are presented in terms of commerce – Healthcare is critical to commerce and worker productivity.

If we look at the ratio of Gross Domestic Product (GDP) to employee pay, related to recessions and political Administration, we can clearly see that since the 2nd year of the Nixon Administration, wages have been falling as a percentage of GDP. This decreased ration does not necessarily reflect a problem, if anything it might suggest a steady increase in productivity and efficiency. As perverse as it might seem, this downward change coincided with the signing of legislation limiting cigarette advertisements – which began the downward trend in smoking and possibly an increase in American health.

Of course, no single factor could decisively account for such

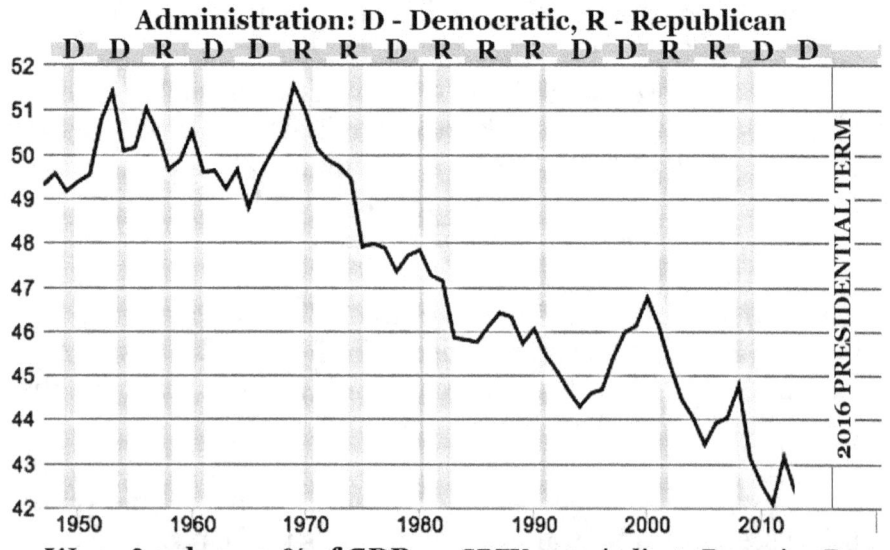

Administration: D - Democratic, R - Republican

Wage & salary as % of GDP.   GREY areas indicate Recession Eras

a steady tread. The 1970's also marked the beginning of the modern tread toward personal computerization.

Some might want to attribute any productivity gains to the introduction of pagers, or mobile phones. While the mobile phone (forerunner to cellphones) has been around since Professor Albert Jahnke developed one in 1908, it wasn't until Amos E. Joel, Jr., a Bell Labs engineer, invented a "three-sided trunk circuit," in 1970, that the "call handoff" process from one cell to another made the units practical. Thus we have another technology which certainly influenced the interaction between the GDP, individual wages, and business efficiency.

In terms of recessions, there is a general pattern indicating that, for the years represented here, they are relatively independent of political Administration – occurring roughly every ten years and indicating that we can expect one in the second term of whoever is elected in 2016.

We can speak in terms of the Four Horseman, who emerged when the Fourth Seal was broken. We also know the Red Horseman has an appointment to finish his war (or begin an new one) between 2013 and 2015. Once his role is completed, the Fifth Seal must be broken.

When he had opened the fifth seal, I saw under the altar the souls of them that were killed for the word of God, and for the testimony which they maintained. And they cried with a loud voice, saying, How long, Lord, holy and true! Doest not thou judge and avenge our blood on them that dwell on the earth? And long white robes were given unto every one, and it was said unto them, that they should rest for a little season until their fellow servants, and their brethren that should be killed even as they were, were fulfilled. [6:9-11]

Those who will be given the "long white robes" are waiting for revenge through the judgment of those who killed them. We might say they are awaiting justice, but must await a natural death, or the killing, of their compatriots. Those whose deeds inflict harm on their fellow humans are certainly not among those who survive.

Lawmakers have a chance to raise the standards of living for many people. Do they really want to go down divided and spitting falsehoods? Granted, those lies and the associated empty rhetoric fulfills the basic requirement for mid-term election victory in states where the common voter noted for their propensity to consistently vote against their own self-interest.

Those who truly believe in the truth of prophecy need quickly realize the Tea Party is the agent of divine wrath. But they also can see the timelines indicate Hitler was also an agent of wrath, and that the system is structured to ensure the just self-identify through the rejection of those divine agents. Universally, scriptures argue for the rejection of evil, and for demonstrating the way you wished to be treated via the way you treat your neighbors and strangers.

In 2014, Americans will determine the treatment they will accept from foreign powers. If they hold that the sick should be allowed to fend for themselves, then, should the nation suffer an earthquake – the next 'big one' due in California, or a repeat to the 22 March 1816 New Madrid, Missouri quake, which ran church bells in Boston – would the nation be worthy of international assistance? Or should it be left to fend for itself?

While individual charities have demonstrated their belief in assisting others, attacks on Obamacare indicate that Caesar – the nation as a whole – is being challenged for wanting to make it part of the national character, or official American morality.

In an article dated 24 October 2013, The Iowa Republican declared, "Make no mistake; it is the personal impact that ObamaCare will have on women, seniors, and families that is the real trainwreck for Democratic candidates who have tied themselves to the unpopular law.

They then predicted: In Iowa:

– Health care costs for individual market plans will increase 10%.

– Seniors will see Medicare cuts to doctors and hospitals totaling more than $10,000 per Iowa enrollee.

– A 27 year old will see their premiums increase by 12% and a 50 year old by more than 13% according to the Heritage Foundation.

The honesty of their prediction might well be declared a factor in the outcome of the Senate race between Republican Mark Jacobs and Democrat Bruce Braley, where Jacobs stated:

"Bruce Braley promised Obamacare would be "good for Iowa." As one of this failed policy's strongest supporters, Braley even delivered the closing arguments for Obamacare on the House floor. And when the truth came out that Obamacare would negatively impact 27,000 Iowa jobs and hurt Iowa families through reduced work hours, lost wages, higher employee contributions, and in some cases, outright cancellation of healthcare plans, Bruce Braley didn't blink. ... Bruce Braley has failed to stand up for Iowa families. And now he wants a promotion? Iowans don't need another career politician embracing this Administration's failed policies." [6 February 2014]

In terms of the 'End-of-Times' prophecy, standard political rhetoric becomes a matter of truth or deception – with the deceivers representing the agents of Divine Wrath intent upon the destruction of a third to a half of the population. The only issue is whether that destruction refers to the Christian, National, or Global population.

"*Saint Paul's Joke,*" we can focus the prophecy on a Gentile-Christian population specifically because they willfully and with forethought violate the teachings and Doctrinal Premise of St. Paul. We know their scripture asserts Jesus saying he will be rejecting some who falsely come in "His Name," because he does not have a basis for knowing them – that is, they follow neither the teachings of Peter, or of Paul.

Fortunately, most people reject this idea – but that forms the basis for the prophetic aspect of the rejection and its applicability to this point in history. Those who assert belief must also reject the doctrines and prophecies which form the basic tenets of their faith.

At its core, the logical problem is circular. Those who assert their belief must act against the tenets of that belief – or prophecy cannot be fulfilled.

In Iowa, the Affordable Care Act is presented as a horror, in

Maine, the insurer that has enrolled the most customers isn't the state's well-established Blue Cross Blue Shield, rather it is Maine Community Health Options, a startup that didn't exist in 2010, but was created under Obamacare.

Iowa style health law opponents predicted insurance co-ops would fail, and the funds they were loaned to get off the ground would be lost. Instead, by 2014, nationally twenty-three co-ops had come into existence, with a health plan enrolled providing 300,000 people with low premium coverage with ample funds to repay the startup costs.

The loans are divided into two segments, roughly 16 percent covers start-up expenses and hiring staff – this is to be repaid in 5 years – the balance, repaid in 15 years, covers the state regulatory requirements for insurers' financial reserves.

In this case, the term "co-op" is actually an anagram for what the 2010 Patient Protection and Affordable Care Act referred to as "Consumer Operated and Oriented Plans."

To be accurate, early computer glitches have caused some co-ops (Maryland) to face initial struggles; while other co-ops have hampered themselves (Michigan and Tennessee) by initially setting their premiums high – but successful co-ops have emerged as price leaders, and have proven to be responsible for over a third of the lowest-premium plans offered. In Wisconsin, customers are drawn to the nonprofit, member-governed business model which defines Obamacare and conforms to the Midwestern tradition of consumer driven control.

Co-op success includes innovative benefit features that offer free doctors' visits and generic drugs, and even $100 gift cards for people who get an annual physical.

In March 2014, the problem which seemed to be emerging was not one of fail, but success. In Iowa, CoOportunity, which also serves Nebraska, projected it's end of March enrollment would be 11,800, but by mid-March it had already enrolled 54,000, and this opens the possibility they could run afoul of state regulatory cash reserve requirements. This then allows opponents – any elected to power in 2014 – to sabotage an emerging and successful privatized healthcare program and achieve the goal of denial of health services to one in six Americans.

In terms of prophecy, they need then double that level to achieve the required third of population levels mandated by the pouring out of the fifth vial and the subsequent making the kingdom wax dark, while its subjects gnaw their tongues in sorrow as they engage in blasphemy against heaven. [16:10-11]

Once the groundwork is set by the 2014 mid-term election, power to attack Obamacare, and every beneficial program which serves to shape the American economy, will then be established or refuted.

Note that the period 2013 to 2015 is a critical year for the Red Horseman – with emphasis on 2015, the year a new American Congress assumes the clear power to support or refute Obama.

If established, the new Congress – a Republican controlled House and Senate – will then pass legislation that President Obama will veto; they will not have the majority necessary to override and so the program will continue. Congress will then play budgetary games to hamper Obamacare and the nation in 2016 – the result will be a 2017 recession which will make a mockery of the one in 2007.

Who will be the President?

Among the Republicans, Ted Cruz is a natural born Canadian and therefore Constitutionally ineligible for office – his nomination alone would broadcast a total disregard for the Constitution among the Tea Party Republicans, and the Republican Party as a whole.

Chris Christie of New Jersey has ben suggested, but the facts associated with his administration of power within that sate has revealed he is more overtly questionable than either Richard Nixon or Spiro Agnew.

Among, Democrats Hillary Clinton appears to be frontrunner and a viable woman to be first female American President – yielding a second consecutive first, and finalization of goals set down by civil rights activists in the 1960's (but it is unlikely she will run, or if she did, would not be sidelined by a medical issue). If we consider that The Tea Party represents the Dragon of *Revelation*, than it could be that in this passage might refer to Clinton:

> And when the dragon saw that he was cast unto the earth, he persecuted the woman which had brought forth the man child. But to the woman were given two wings of a great Eagle, that she might fly into the wilderness, into her place, where she is nourished for a time, and times, and half a time, from the presence of the serpent. [12:13-14]

On Thursday, 6 March 2014, Ted Cruz drew cheers by saying: "We need to repeal every single word of Obamacare!"

The goal is to deprive Americans of affordable medical care, and it is cheered by those who seek to harm their countrymen – thereby renouncing the lesson to be derived by the Good Samaritan parable, and thus a mandate of Jesus. The act of doing so thereby disqualifies them from any benefits they might seek by assert the name of Jesus in their defense.

Obviously the serpent needs to attack the lady nd the male she 'creates'. The phrase used, "time, and times, and half a time," is generally taken to mean a period of 42-months, or 3.5 years.

In February 2014, The Blaze reported Ted Cruz saying that has been "consistently wrong" on both foreign policy and domestic policy; that her 1990's healthcare proposals "would have been every bit as disastrous as Obamacare"; that, as Secretary of State, she was responsible for "alienating allies and cozying up to enemies."

A corresponding Reuters' story has Cruz saying: "Let's look at the last 40 years. Every single time Republicans have nominated a presidential candidate who ran as a strong conservative, we won. And every time we have nominated a candidate who ran as an establishment moderate, we lost."

In those terms, a Tea Party Conservative will most likely be the one to represent the Republicans in 2016; therefore, assuming Republican control of both Houses of Congress, the United States will produce unrestricted legislation designed to cripple Education, Social Security and anything deemed to be "welfare."

Money
Importance of 2014 election

Ted Cruz has said he would remain neutral during the 2014 Congressional primary contests: "I'm not supporting any of the senators in my party or their opponents. I'm leaving it to the grass roots to make their decision."

As we know, Cruz has also pointed out that, "Every single time Republicans have nominated a presidential candidate who ran as a strong conservative," they successfully won control of the White House. But what does it mean to be "conservative"?

If the "conservative" term refers to fiscal behavior, and that refers to deficit spending – living beyond one's income or means – than the United States ceased being "conservative" around 1970.

It was in 1970 that American deficits went out of control; it was also in 1970 that the concept of Credit Cards came to dominate the social-economic landscape.

In terms of credit mentality: the first plastic Diner Club Card was introduced in 1961 – the card itself having been introduced in 1950, followed by the American Express Card. The first Playboy Club opened in Chicago, in February 1960, as an extension of the private club mentality; in 1963, credit was defined in terms of the Danny Kaye movie, "The Man from Diners Club." Comedy aside, the idea of a multipurpose charge card as originally conceived as a means of avoiding the embarrassment caused by having too little cash in ones wallet – it was something to be paid in full at the end of the month. Credit represented cash in the bank and a utilitarian monthly utility bill.

The very idea of credit, or general credit, went contrary to the conservative financial immigrant mentality defined by those who had arrived in America from the late 1800's through the 1940's. Throughout the history of America, deficits were accompanied by an expectation of revenues in the immediate future – only during the Civil War, when [illegal] income taxes were first introduced, was there any real deficit spending. Ignoring the reality that we are no longer an agrarian culture, many "conservatives" seek to abandon the Income Tax structure introduced in 1913 – when they should be adjusting it to reflect a twenty-first century "software substitution" culture. But modern Conservatives are Luddites addicted to debt.

Consider where a "software substitution" paradigm is already leading society – Several automobile manufactures now offer auto-park feature.

Imagine being able to parallel park at the push of a button. or possibly getting into the passenger seat of your car and simply telling it where you want to go. Not only will the walls and roads have ears, but the vehicles and appliances will be listening better than any spouse – and probably responding better too.

Is our society going to be ready for a world where people do not need to work?

Sure, people will work. But not at traditional drudgery which replaced the classical drudgery of daily backbreaking labor. Think about how long it has been since advanced cultures were forced to do the type of labor involved in pyramid construction; how long since we needed to build a Stonehenge in order to have an accurate calendar?

If we wish to witness unnecessary hardship, we can look at Third World cultures. But even the Third World is leapfrogging into the twenty-first century through the widespread use of cellphones and the internet. Unfortunately, while technology can easily destroy nature, it has not yet reached the point where advanced societies are willing to devote the intellectual effort required to ensure reliable sources of clean water and arable land – that awaits a final pouring out of the Seven Vials and the death of a third of the people.

It is all about money.

We have a culture dominated by people who are devoted to the accumulation of pieces of paper, while espousing adherence to religions which advocate against "monetary wealth."

Over the past century, the American Income Tax system has evolved into a structure devoted to transferring money from the low level worker to the upper 1-percent. Conceptually, it has become the democratic equivalent of a monarchy. Those who are part of the nobility are assured the wealth will gravitate toward them. But that is not going to work when "software substitution" begins to facilitate the advance of intellect – the type of structure which was built into the biblical Israelite marriage code, a structure where intellect is rewarded and inheritance reflects a genetic inheritance of IQ over the territorially confining base inheritance of the lower "Tribes."

The concept of "software substitution" has begun to enter the arena of "wearable software." In terms of the American Tax Code, your clothes will soon become your office and therefore your daily wardrobe will become a fully tax deductible business expense.

Consider our social welfare programs – Obamacare, Food Stamps, Low Income Energy Assistance, Section 8 Housing, Social Security, pensions and disability.

Consider these "archaic" programs in terms of a culture with 3D-printers which are cheaper than many regular printers were in the 1980's. Consider the world when these printers are capable of organic printing – the creation of human organs based on a genetic sample of the recipient and therefore eliminating the need for third-party donors. Think about this: 3D-printers are already taking on elements of a *Star Trek* replicator.

If we think in terms of "wearable software," aren't we really talking about computers, phones, and entertainment systems being built into something we not only can wear on a daily basis, but can toss in the washing machine – unless it takes the form of a piece of jewelry.

Back in 1960, I studied electronics in High School. There I learned about wartime "razor blade" radios and rectifier circuits; I put them together to create a wireless battery which was useless because of the relatively enormous power needs of transistors and diode circuits. Now the same circuit generates relatively enormous amounts of power relative to the needs of an integrated circuit.

Built into a wearable, the circuit I designed in 1960 would, in the presence of any type of radio, TV or Wi-Fi signal, easily power a cellphone, or tablet computer, without a battery, though it would probably be more efficient to use the circuit to constantly charge an internal trickle-charge-battery style circuit.

If we think in terms of self-parking, self-driving vehicles, why not self-operating (possibly self-powered) construction and farming equipment? The only thing a human would need do is provide the blueprint, design or planting instructions.

In terms of my energy-from-the-air design, it only took fifty-years to move from impractical to highly possible. It took thirty-five years to move from the first clumsy PC to tablet computers which have more power than the 1970's IBM mainframes – which cost a million dollars, occupied whole floors in major office buildings and required their own air conditioning systems (aside from still being programmed and operated with the type of punch cards once used to control weaving looms).

In the thirty years since their introduction in 1983, mobile phones went from bulky boxes to something that could fit into the coin pocket of a business suit; with the Internet following ten years later and then becoming compatible enough to allow, for practical purposes, the average person to view their phone as their computer.

When Ted Cruz speaks of "conservative," is he speaking of a person who is out of touch with reality – a Luddite? Or someone who understands exactly how quickly the world is changing and is ready to apply traditional, tried and true, universal standards to the creation of a modern society?

Does "conservative" mean being like Ronald Reagan, George H. W. Bush, and George Bush – each of whom doubled the national debit without producing any concrete social benefits? Or does it mean being a Bill Clinton style "tax and spend" leader who proved to be capable of both reducing the national debit, and producing a budgetary surplus?

Looking at the charts reveals the pattern of recession and the United States Federal Deficits as a percent of its GDP. The upper chart covers the period from the Kennedy Era, while the lower chart reveals the deficit pattern over the past century. We should note a significant change from the 1900 Republican Era: Those states which voted Republican in 1900 now are considered Democratic. In 1900 William McKinley became President, with Teddy Roosevelt as his VP – becoming President a year later, after Pres. McKinley was assassinated. He was the succeeded by William Howard Taft, a Republican whose victory would now be attributed to Democratic states, but then were States with high immigrant populations.

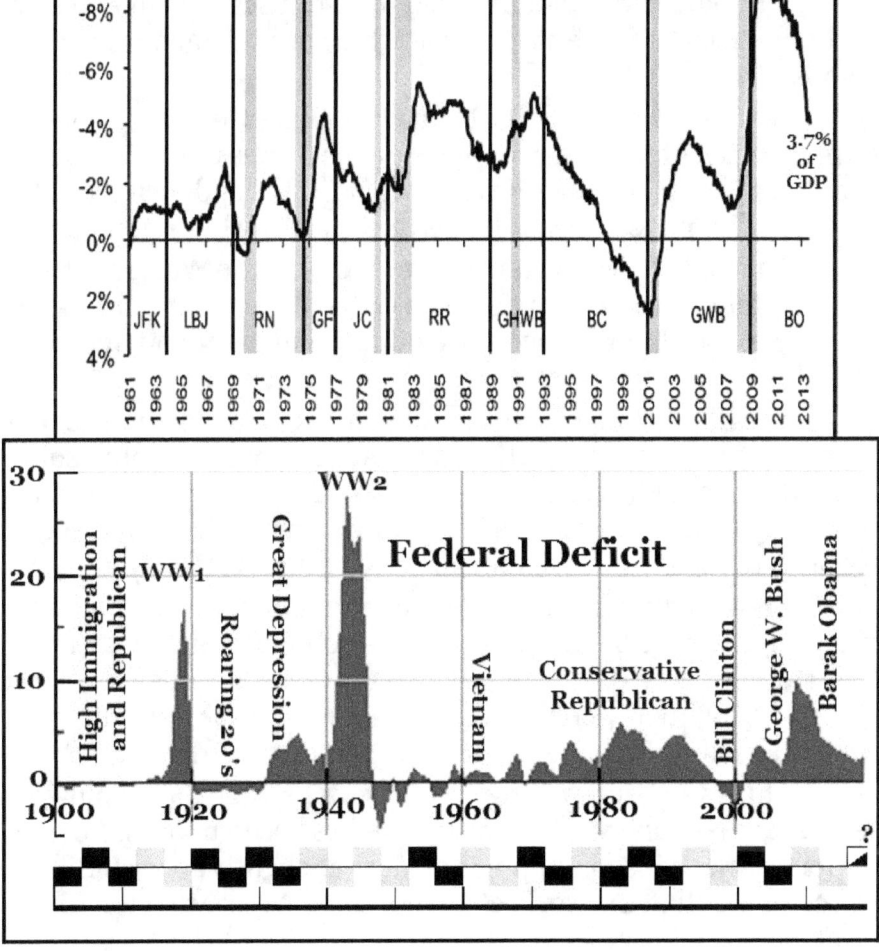

The Great Depression and World War Two appear to have changed everything for the nation, with the Korean War accounting for the deficit during the first Eisenhower administration. Once the nation became involved in Vietnam – under Eisenhower, with the successive pattern of escalation until the ignominious withdrawal during the Nixon Administration – deficits and military incursions became the pattern associated with Republican administrations.

Conservative Republicans win elections, become engaged in military conflicts marked by the United States being the aggressor, and create enormous deficits. If we look to the Roaring Twenties, we see a Republican period marked by surpluses and an excessive use of financial leverage akin to that which brought about the 2007 collapse.

We know from our charts that the White Horseman appears with the onset of the Great Depression, and rides until the 2007/8 Recession. We could safely assert that both the deficits and the nature of the modern Republicans are related to his emergence.

The Red Horseman emerges to bring us into World War Two and the Holocaust, and carries us into the pre-election 2015 issues with the associated re-emergence of anti-Semitism and attacks of both Kosher slaughter and circumcision.

The Black Horseman coincides with Richard Nixon and then the formation of the allegedly Conservative Republican philosophy typified by Ronald Reagan and the "Reagan Republicans" who are now being attacked by the Tea Party Movement – which followed on the heels of the Pale Horseman and a voice among the Four Beasts.

Between 1971 and 2007, Money and commerce, with a saving of the oil, becomes the focus of political action and deficit creation. As history informs us, this period begins with the Consumer Price Index at roughly 6-percent and climbing to 12-percent after the 1974 Arab Oil Embargo – *"... and oil, and wine hurt thou not."*

Things get interesting when we take a global population perspective – as in the next chart, which is based upon the United Nations projections fo a population decline slightly above 8 Billion, and estimates that the world could not sustain more that ten Billion people.

By the time of the Trumpets, a third of the trees and all of the green grass shall be burnt; a third of the creatures of the sea shall die, a third of ships destroyed; a third of rivers and fountains burn and are wormwood (poisoned); a third of the sun, moon, and stars are darkened (?air pollution?); a third of men are slain.

Finally, there are horses with heads of lions and these were *the third part of men killed, that is, of the fire, and of the smoke, and of the brimstone.* [9:18] And yet there would still be those who would not repent their murder, sorcery, fornication and theft.

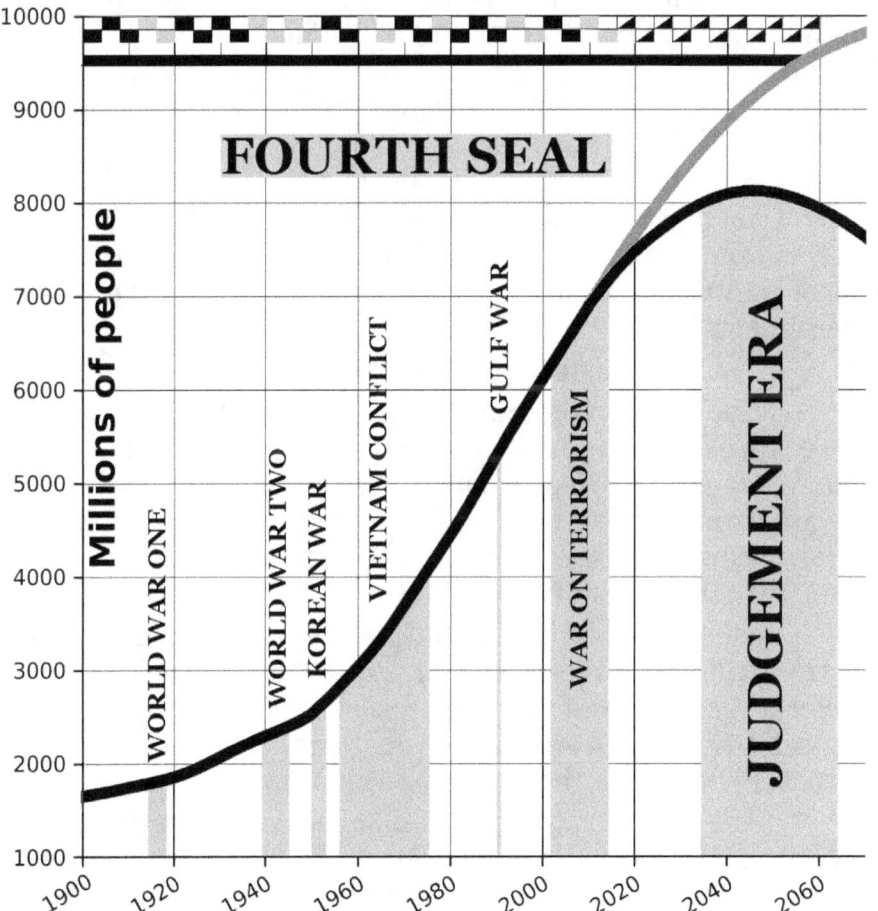

Do we need to rely upon ancient prophecy in order to accept what is being said by modern science?

Polluted air, soil and water are to kill off a third of humanity.

There are to be plagues and wars which will bring about the death of many. To believe this, or reject it, only requires we look around and decide what we wish to promote.

For the United States – which might possibly be *Babylon the great city*, which is to fall, *for she made all nations to drink of the wine of the wrath of her fornication [14:8]* – the destruction is one of political choice.

Throughout the twentieth century, it has been United States policy to interject itself into the internal affairs of other nations. In 2014, it decided to repudiate or invalidate a Crimean separatist vote which saw 95.7-percent of Crimean residents declare they wished to be part of Russia rather than the Ukraine.

Were we looking at a Republican White House, history infers there would be a move toward some form of military intervention. But that would mean a direct confrontation with Russia, on Russian soil, or within easy retaliatory range of the full might of the Russian government.

In this case, history grants us an interesting perspective.

As far back as a Scythian face-off against the Persian empire – 26 centuries ago – the ancestors of the Rus refrained from attack; rather they allowed their enemy to come to them. As we come forward in time, we see they did this with Napoleon, and then with Hitler. They make their enemy – who is the aggressor – come to them for the honor of dying.

In the words of the ancient Greek Oracle, "The first one into the river will lose." This is a lesson which Germany failed to learn in World War One, and was reminded of in the Second War; it is a lesson North Korea learned; one America should have learned in Vietnam. Ultimately, the aggressor will always lose.

If America extends itself – without having first suffered some form of Pearl Harbor – it cannot hope to remain intact. It is both ancient wisdom and, apparently, divine prophecy.

Climate Change
One of many prophetic givens

Dr. Mario J. Molina report to American Association for the Advancement of Science, establishes that the human emissions of heat-trapping gases are already being felt, and that the ultimate consequences could be dire. Those who acknowledge the melting of the glacial icecaps already know the reality – then there are those who prefer to deny reality.

Their pattern of denial carries over into other aspects of reality, and are represented by both the American voting patterns and attitudes toward science – such as the ability of an original deity to design a system based on evolution. As we know from Creationism, there is an element of American culture which denies their deity has that capability.

The report stated, "The evidence is overwhelming: Levels of greenhouse gases in the atmosphere are rising." But the report, entitled "*What we Know*," does not overwhelm with science, rather it deals with basic reality and facts which are agreed upon by 97-percent of climate scientists – the remaining 3-percent still have some questions they need answered before assigning significant blame on human activities.

In terms of prophecy, the Talmud claims 1.2 million prophets in the period between the two Holy Temples (967bce-69ce). During that period, there were academies or schools dedicated to helping men and women cross the spiritual threshold which would afford them access to apparently supernatural knowledge and information which we sometimes refer to as prophecy. In a secular context, that prophecy is prediction – and the predictions are far more specific.

If we look at Revelation 5:6, we are told of these prophets as being "the voice of many Angels round about the throne, and about the beasts and the Elders, and there were ten thousand times ten thousand," or 100 million, plus another "thousand thousands." In a sense, the voices account for all the Israelites who might ever have lived, plus all those Gentiles who followed the teaching of Paul until the age of Augustine when Christians became Romans, and Jesus was formally changed into a Herculean deity.

Maimonides defined eleven forms of prophecy, generalizing the practice in these terms:

"The spirit of prophecy only rests upon the wise – on those who are distinguished by great wisdom and strong moral character, whose passions never overcome them in anything whatsoever, but who by their rational faculty always have their passions under control and possess broad and calm minds."

Prophecy, the ability to predict a future event, is universal and natural; it is also something which a third of people close their minds to – even when confronted by the physical realities that the predictions are true.

Some might shake their heads in disagreement – they can be seen to represent the third – but most people accept the rational. The idea of climate change is denied, yet icecaps are still melting.

As stated earlier in this book, prophecy is little more than prediction based on repetitive patterns of behavior. The patterns of behavior are both natural (environmental) and human behavioral consistency.

If a prophecy refers to events in a distant future, the specifics are vague and symbolic. As the events begin to come together, it is easier to distinguish the critical elements and so you can move from the realm of prophecy to that of prediction. And then there is the realm of reality – those who are looking and those who are not: or, as it is phrased, those with the 'eyes to see and hears to hear' and those who select to wear blindfolds, place their fingers in their ears, and run around making sounds to further mask what is said.

In the post-war consumer era which defined the Vietnam era, chlorofluorocarbons were utilized in refrigerators, air-conditioners, cans of hair spray and deodorant. It wasn't until the 1970's that scientists discovered they were accumulating in the air and breaking down the ozone layer – the a blanket of atmospheric gas protecting the world from lethal exposure to ultraviolet radiation.

There is a somewhat delicate, self-adjusting, balance between the various gases and chemicals which are naturally released into the atmosphere. Humans have reached a stage in their evolution where they have disrupted that balance through the use of what are generally termed fossil fuels, and concentrated chemicals – like chlorofluorocarbons.

In *Revelation*, the application of chemicals is termed, '*vials of wrath*'. The ancient prophet did not need to know about specific chemicals, nor did he need to know anything about those things we now classify as science. All that was required was to look out the window in any non-Israelite city, or Gentile district within a city and he would see human waste poured into the streets, rivers and onto the land. He could pass a shop and see waste products dumped into pools that everyone knew were then deadly.

All that was necessary for a prophecy to become true was to extrapolate a larger population. When the Book of Revelation was written, Rome was the largest known city – a city composed of five story concrete buildings, and having a population of one million people. Moreover, it was literally a pigsty. And it was seen as worse by one who actually followed a religion which mandated cleanliness.

Anyone who remembers the 1980 TV mini-series, "*Shogun*," might recall the sequences in which the Europeans are repulsed by the Japanese habit of routinely bathing, or taking their shoes off at the door so as not to track in dirt. Eventually, the primary character – Pilot John Blackthorne – become acclimated to the customs and strips away a jacket he was wearing when he realizes it had picked up a flea after he visited residence housing the surviving members of his crew.

Factually, there was a period in history in which Europeans believed dirt to be healthy and washing (cleanliness) caused disease. For those who knew better, it was easy to prophesy about plague. It actually becomes easier, when you realize that theirs was the same thinking now associated with Creationism. This is the same thinking which denies the Holocaust, denies climate change, denies healthcare to the sick – or for whom any illness would have a most devastating on themselves and those dependant upon them.

Politically, these are the people who would deny that global Temperatures are rising; that Springs are arriving earlier; that ice sheets are melting; that Sea level is rising; and that the patterns of rainfall and drought are changing.

In accordance with prophecy, both natural precipitation, and human travel, patterns have shifted in a way which allows tropical disease to move northward into regions where there are no natural defenses. Also in terms of prophecy, the oceans are acidifying – a vial of wrath has been poured into them by chemical realignments related to the melting ice caps. As a result, the patterns of illness will change and those who were predicted to serve "the dragon" or "serpent" will oppose people the idea of medical care – the Good Samaritan type of care which does not first check a person's wallet.

Let's into another context – the change from Republican to Democrat which accompanied and followed America being dragged into World War Two.

Prior to the War, Prescott Bush – father to George H. W. And grandfather to George W. – helped finance the Nazi Party through an investment bank that operated as a clearing house for many assets and enterprises held by German steel magnate Fritz Thyssen.

In theory, Prescott was not a Nazi sympathizer; in theory, according to Ted Cruz's father, Barack Obama is said to have been born in Kenya – both theories seem to lack concrete evidence, and actually go against known facts.

It is claimed that, as a member of Yale's secretive *Skull and Crossbones Society*, Prescott Bush proudly desiccated Geronimo's grave and made off with his skull – an act commonly referred to as grave robbing. In many ways, Prescott Bush and his descendants symbolize the Republican Party mindset of the time, and that of The Tea Party Movement leading into the 2014 election.

When the Federal government intervened, Bush turned from passively profiting from facilitating the Nazi war effort, to working with the American Birth Control League and assisting with the capitalization of Planed Parenthood – the antitheses of the Right to Life movement – two operations which are now viewed as clearly part of the Democratic Party philosophy, and marking a change in political philosophy for someone whose family is identified with the Republican Party.

As part of his 1944 State of the Union address, Democratic President Franklin D. Roosevelt proposed a "Second Bill of Rights," because the first ten amendments to the Constitution had "proved inadequate to assure us equality in the pursuit of happiness."

In the spirit of prophecy, Roosevelt stated that America's place in the world would depend upon whether these and similar rights were placed into practice. The rights in question are the same ones being which are emerging as part of the 2014 political debate:

- The right to a useful and remunerative job in the industries or shops or farms or mines of the nation;
- The right to earn enough to provide adequate food and clothing and recreation;
- The right of every farmer to raise and sell his products at a return which will give him and his family a decent living;
- The right of every businessman, large and small, to trade in an atmosphere of freedom from unfair competition and domination by monopolies at home or abroad;
- The right of every family to a decent home;
- The right to adequate medical care and the opportunity to achieve and enjoy good health;
- The right to adequate protection from the economic fears of old age, sickness, accident, and unemployment;
- The right to a good education.
- All of these rights spell security. And after this war is won we must be prepared to move forward, in the implementation of these rights, to new goals of human happiness and well-being.

Look at the sixth "Right" presented in Roosevelt's 11 January 1944 address to the nation – "The right to adequate medical care and the opportunity to achieve and enjoy good health." In many ways, that sounds like *The Affordable Care Act*, Medicaid, Medicare – or the right of someone to be healthy enough to work, and to have their family healthy, so as not to create emotional distractions from work. Something we know for a fact is opposed by The Tea Party Movement, and the absence of which ensures the fulfillment of prophecies related to plague and famine.

Climate change isn't just a matter of changes in the physical environment, it is also a matter of the political climate – a climate that flipped during the Second World War and turned Democrats into Republicans and Republicans into Democrats, while allowing those who most often waved the Bible to remain those who most opposed its teachings.

As Roosevelt correctly pointed out "All of these rights spell security." Obviously, if we undermine personal security, we also undermine national security, and that brings us to a March 2014 report on a study derived from the "Human And Nature Dynamical" model devised by applied mathematician Safa Motesharri – funded by NASA's Goddard Space Flight Center with subsequent publican in the Ecological Economics journal.

In accordance with the pattern of prophecy premise of this book, the study referred to sophisticated civilizations – the Roman, Han and Gupta Empires for example – which were sophisticated and collapsed. The idea of a "conservative" approach to political matters reflects the classic "business as usual" approach typical of societies which ignore warnings of disaster until it is too late.

Motesharri acknowledged: "the process of rise-and-collapse is actually a recurrent cycle found throughout history," and that the convergence of climate change and population growth can stretch resources to the point of collapse – projected to start about 2029.

This would then infer that The Tea Party republicans have a pattern based statistical probability of rationally disproportionate victory in the 2014 American mid-term elections. Once they have achieved their victory, and with two years to solidify the destruction of the United States, the 2016 Presidential contest could easily go to the Democratic candidate.

Way of Thinking
Meaningless stuff

Consider the possibility that there are two kinds of threats which would conform to prophecy. First there is the climate change collectively caused to the biosphere by human behavior; then we have the enormous vulnerability created by egotistical political acts in response to irrelevant foreign realignments.

Ours is an interconnected world; one which became more so after the Second World War. The fear of "Communism," and the fall of status among those who deem themselves "Elite," transformed what could be considered Christian mandate, and the policies of the "Second Bill of Rights," into 'socialism' which was to be rejected.

As a result, anytime a politician wants to generate knee-jerk opposition, they need only label something 'socialist' – even though it is actually beneficial within a long-term capitalist context. The need to generate opposition comes from the political need for a short-term benefit – immediate electoral support, or ballot cast.

Short-term political impatience, which grows from a need for immediate gratification on the part of the electorate, brings about errors in global political judgment – the Vietnam Conflict was just such an error.

In the 1968, Jeffrey Simon – currently an Adjunct Senior Research Fellow in the Institute for National Strategic Studies at the National Defense University – summarized the situation perfectly: if the United States simply distributed the funds being spent on the military in Vietnam, among its citizens, it would be the third richest economy in the world and would have no reason to go Communist.

Conflicts are generally derived from an imbalance between the 'Elite' consumption levels and the resources remaining for the 'Masses.'

The economic collapse model devised by Motesharri found that civilization "appears to be on a sustainable path for quite a long time, but even using an optimal depletion rate and starting with a very small number of 'Elites', these 'Elites' eventually consume too much, resulting in a famine among the Masses that eventually causes the collapse of society."

It is a simple matter of "the economic stratification of society into 'Elites' and 'Masses'." In the real world, it falls upon the 'Elites' to take action to restore the economic balance. According to the Motesharri model, "Collapse can be avoided and population can reach equilibrium if the per capita rate of depletion of nature is reduced to a sustainable level, and if resources are distributed in a reasonably equitable fashion."

If we place that into the current American context, minimum wage rates have fallen below poverty – in the Roosevelt model, the average low level worker can no longer "earn enough to provide adequate food and clothing and recreation." They must therefore rely upon 'welfare' within a society which routinely condemns those who receive such benefits as lazy and undeserving of assistance.

It is interesting that the latter classification is devoutly anti-Christian. Therefore it is espoused by those who, biblically, are to come in the name of Jesus, but who will be unknown to him.

The structure of "The Judgement" is such that it has every individual determine their status through their deeds: the Right-to-Life advocate who declares the mother can die, rather than abort the fetus (which will then also die), has said they have judged and would arbitrarily murder an adult woman they do knot know. As we know, the U.S. Supreme Court declared that was immoral and therefore illegal; so Right-to-Life advocates found another way to achieve the goal, they oppose affordable healthcare, a minimum wage increase and every item enumerated in Roosevelt's "*Second Bill of Rights*."

Right-to-Life advocates are typical of those in the public who are in denial about scenarios that have not yet happened – for the supposedly moral crowd, it is the evidence to be used on *Judgment Day*; for everyone else, it is a combination of history and the causal consequence of their ignorance of that history.

America needs politicians who exercise rational approaches

to low-risk events that carry devastating high-risk consequences – instead their focus is on short-term political solutions to long-term problems.

Consider what would happen if Right-to-Life advocates were able to cause every fetus which will be aborted to be born. Each of them will need pre-natal and post natal care – plus their mothers will need a place to live, proper nutrition, utilities paid, and their own medical care. Subsequently, those mothers will need eighteen years of support – does it matter if it is guaranteed employment, or welfare, they still need the place and ability to raise that child. This is a direct consequences of demands of Right-to-Life advocates, and so falls under their moral responsibility – it is said in many cultures, "If you save a life, you are thereafter responsible for it."

When one nation interjects itself into the internal affairs of another, it is responsible for the consequences. The problem is, many nations have leaders who posture for the sake of appearances – as a result they engage in a game of brinkmanship. The game is safe, when both parties have equal room to retreat, and supply lines which are equally elastic to allow both to advance half way into the other's 'personal space.'

History reveals that China has never extended itself more than half the distance of its secure territory. Only the Mongols, who were not Chinese, ever attempted a further extension of their power and influence. It could be argued that the Romans attempted the same feat of expansion, but the physical extent of their empire was minor by comparison.

Russia learned from the Scythian so would never invade, but quickly fill a power vacuum; but if any are foolish enough to attack them, they retreat in a fashion which forces the aggressor to outrun their lines of supply. Once the enemy has fully stretched the elastic, it is cut and they are crushed.

In the modern world, everything is part of an interconnected global system of banking, power, food supply and consumer basics where any disruption means trouble and sabotage of supply lines is relatively simple. Nations depend on each other to finance deficits and, as with the ancient Egyptians in the time of Joseph, we do not stockpile food – so are unprepared for events which impose famine.

For the first time in its history, the world is primed for the arrival of the Four Horseman and the pouring out of the Seven Vials of Divine Wrath. It is a world where brinkmanship is a fools game, and Chinese-Scythian strategy has the advantage.

It is estimated that the United States has sufficient resources to sustain a 48-hour disruption of international commerce; reality would indicate various regions could manage a week or more before any real deprivation would be felt. We no longer require a nuclear attack – an efficient series of coordinated terrorist assaults on fuel sources and key communication points would be far more efficient.

The prophecies open the door to fulfillment via pandemics accelerated by global air travel, bioterrorist attacks, cyber-attacks on critical infrastructure and computers with artificially intelligence of the type associated with "software substitution."

A major nation, or superpower, no longer needs 'boots on the ground' to sever the critical supply lines of an enemy – consider the simple effect of an oil embargo like that imposed under the Carter Administration, except with hostile intent.

Climate change opens the possibility of global temperatures reaching a tipping point after which feedback effects cause it to get warmer and warmer. Curiously, that would make the United States more secure – it would decrease its dependence on heating fuel and expand the viability of solar and wind as power sources. But that assumes politicians will embrace the latter in the same way they are being adopted in Europe.

Scythian tactics, as used on Napoleon and Hitler, are applied in the winter, at a time when your target is reliant upon stockpiles; a polar vortex would offer the ideal background for sabotaging the energy, communication, and power grid in the United States. This would be preceded by, or coincide with, manipulation of the credit market.

This brings us to the Crimea, but with the suggestion that Syria be kept in the back of your mind.

Crimea
Economic Suicide

The Ukraine emerged from the 1991 dissolution of the Soviet Union as a new independent region, and in 2013, it underwent an internal upheaval which was then dubbed the "Euromaidan" – after the Independence Square in Kiev, Maidan Nezalezhnosti.

Reports indicated that a mere 2,000 people were involved, with latter reports stating they were either guided, or led, by neo-Nazi militant fascist groups who opposed a government decision to abandon an Association Agreement with the European Union. Their action was met with passage of a 100-page anti-protest law, which was then repealed two-months later.

An admittedly biased Canadian report denounced what it termed as an imperialist strategy of 'regime change' associated with classic 20th-century United States policy in Vietnam, Iraq, Iran, and attempted in Afghanistan and Pakistan.

The current point of significance here is, the Ukraine is not a member of NATO, despite years of speculation that it was poised to join, in 2013, the government did decide against joining, and therefore it afforded no protective status under the North Atlantic Treaty, Article 5 – more important, the NATO powers have no legal basis for asserting any direct involvement.

In February 2014, a sniper apparently singled out a protester named Joseph Schilling, a 61-year-old Jewish builder – placing a bullet through his head. This, and other actions which could infer the existence of anti-Semitic undertones, served to refute the idea that the protestors were neo-Nazi fascists.

There is little doubt the uprising and regime change were sponsored by those favoring NATO and EU membership, which gives credibility to this reported statement from Russia:

"According to our data, U.S. officials are spending $ 20 million a week for funding, including weapons, the opposition and the rebels. There is information that in the territory of the U.S. embassy being trained militants that they are armed... Today we have to remember the (1994) Budapest Memorandum ... According to this document, Russia and the United States are the guarantors of the sovereignty and territorial integrity of Ukraine and, frankly, are obliged to intervene when there are conflicts of this kind. And the fact that Americans get up today, unilaterally rudely interfering in the internal affairs of Ukraine, – a clear violation of the treaty." Sergei Glazyev, adviser to President Vladimir Putin, February 6, 2014 [1]

The 5 December 1994 Budapest Memorandum – entered into by the Russian Federation, United States of America, and United Kingdom – relates to the Treaty on the Non-Proliferation of Nuclear Weapons, and led to the removal from the Ukraine of what had been the third largest repository of nuclear arms in the world. The idea of NATO membership infers a restoration of those weapons systems and creation of a clear threat to Russia.

Of some significance is the fact that annexation of Crimea by Russia dates back to the 1994 Crimean presidential elections, when Yuriy Meshkov won with 72.9 percent of the vote on a platform dedicated to the Crimea-Russia unification. The following year, on 17 March 1995, the Ukrainian parliament scrapped the Crimean Constitution and abolished the post of president – thus setting the stage for the 2014 events.

In March 2014, Crimeans flocked to vote Crimea separation from the Ukraine. In the first six hours 44.27% had voted in what was called a "record-breaking" turned out. The tallied final votes showed Crimean residents had overwhelmingly voted to secede from the Ukraine and join Russia as expressed by a 97 percent win.

The vote created a celebration akin to the American Fourth of July [Independence Day] – fireworks exploded and Russian flags fluttered above jubilant crowds. Meantime, the United States and Europe condemned the ballot as illegal and destabilizing. While it was pointed out – by the United States – that the vote violated the Ukrainian Constitution, there was a point of humor to the reaction.

In 1776, Colonial actions violated Britain's legal charter.

Russia enters the Crimea, the people shoot off fireworks and cheer; America enters another country, the people curse and shoot the American soldiers – America envies the Russian version.

One issue being raised in America, and particularly among those who align with The Tea Party Movement, is whether or not a free people have the right to vote for independence from a regime which does not represent their interests. Those who feel it is illegal will oppose the overwhelming historical evidence underlying the March 2014 Crimean vote.

Newsnight, a BBC production, aired, "Neo-Nazi threat in new Ukraine," which reveals xenophobic anti-Semite nationalists, armed and led the mobs in Kiev – thus directly contradicting the earlier reports of a movement inspired by individuals asserting freedom, democracy, and closer Western ties. If the United States supports Democracy, then it must recognize the Crimean Separatist vote for which the historic antecedent is firmly established in the 1994 vote, and the possibly illegal action by of the Ukraine abolishing a valid Crimean National Constitution.

Russian entry into Crimea triggered emotional outbursts of frustration, anger and incredulity among some in Washington. It is difficult for policymakers and pundits to constructively address the imagined problems which arise from Russian action, and what appears to have been a democratic vote that is consistent with the desire of the people dating as far back as 1994.

There were those who struggled for a way to blame President Obama for these events, and to find means to exert clandestine pressure upon him to over react to what is actually a simple voter driven change of national affiliation. The complexity, context and background of these events reflects the Russian strategic interests in Crimea.

The actual strategic relationship and interests date back to the time when the Scythians ruled the region – 3500 years ago – and is familiar with any who know the Greek legends of Amazon Warriors who established their community along the Sea of Azov, northeast of the Scythian Crimea and were discovered by Scythian men – who they eventually married as equals.

Historically, Russia is committed to its desire to maintain a warm water port access to the world and this underscores the reality of Russian interests and national security. Economically, Crimea is a solid industrial commercial region and tourist resort destination with its own natural gas and oil field energy resources. Curiously, aside from its physical location, Russia has no real need for the Crimea – the same cannot be said for the Ukraine, and the United States has absolutely no interest there.

The war mongers, those who represent one of the Horsemen, would enjoy seeing Obama take assertive (read: military) action to ostensibly persuade Russia forego its long-standing connection to the region. The United States does not have leverage over Russia – on the contrary, the economic structure of Russia is such that it may have options capable of economically crippling critical segments of the American economy, while violating rational free market policy.

We need only think back to the December 2013 Tea Party effort to collapse the full faith obligation underlying the Treasury Bond debt which represents the American National Debt – a perfectly rational action would be to divest of American securities and seek a new reserve currency.

Internal divisions in Ukraine are historically real and can be expected to endure long after the current situation has faded into history. But in many ways, the Crimea situation is analogous to the Texas and the Alamo, but with some notable differences.

At the time of the Battle of the Alamo, in February 1839, the United States had only existed since the signing of its Constitution in 1787 – less than 52 years. Sam Houston, Davy Crockett and the rest were clearly not ethnic Mexicans – it was a land grab. Those who voted in the Crimea were basically ethnic Russians voting to be re-affiliated with the nation they had been separated from; Crimea was also voting itself away from an unstable and unrelated criminal regime.

We also note that both Texas and Crimea were independent

Republics prior to being absorbed into the alien nation. Given the history of the Alamo and annexation of Texas and the Alamo, it is clear that those who identify as non-native Texans would advocate for the Ukraine – exerting a total disregard for the democratically expressed will of the ancestrally native population. If the pattern repeats, there will be a Black Sea war sometime around 2022, and the American President will represent a Tea Party like group.

As for any concept of US credibility, reality shows that this is more of a conservative think tank and Republican senate delusion than a real world consideration. The US has been working toward the destruction of its credibility since its incursion into Vietnam; the assertions of WMD's and the whole double Iraq War scenarios – which destabilized the only stable government in the region – are evidence that America cannot impose its will on foreign nations.

Pax Americana is a viable concept – if it is accompanied by the realization that, as with the British in 1776, the Spanish-America War of 1898, or the German occupation when faced with resistance forces, America lacks the ability to fight native resistance forces. If America enters a foreign conflict, it must do so as a welcomed guest.

Futile and disruptive US interventionist actions and policies around the world have done nothing to support the concept of US credibility. Where US security is at stake – which is not in Ukraine – the US has consistently demonstrated gross incompetence.

As pointed out by Robert Gates, the Defense Secretary under George W. Bush, "Putin invaded Georgia when George W. Bush was president. Nobody ever accused George W. Bush of being weak or unwilling to use military force." Gates pointed out the importance of Republicans expressing their support for, rather than attacking, President Obama.

On 18 March 2014, Ted Cruz stated:

"The administration has so badly bungled Ukraine and so badly bungled foreign policy for the last five years. Putin's aggression, his act of war against Ukraine, is a direct consequence of the lack of U.S. leadership over the last five years."

We know Cruz's father has stated Obama was a Kenyan and that numerous individuals have consistently asserted that Obama was Constitutionally ineligible to legally hold the office of President. By so doing – without there being any evidence to support a Bill of Impeachment – they have willfully undermined the credibility of the American system. In effect they have asserted to the world that both political parties, but most notably the Republican Party which controls the House of Representatives, and Constitutionally has the obligation to file Impeachment charges, is delict in its duties. That would make the American government, Washington, as criminal and corrupt as any third world dictatorial regime.

The act of attacking the president – even over such trivial things as taking a bit of time off to relax – is undermining the ability of America to assert influence anywhere in the world.

If we look at Russia, which has, for the past half-century been the big bad bogeyman, we see a nation whose troops seem to remain home. We need to assess the basis of Russian power and determine why it is so much different from that demonstrated by America to retain bases around the world – when the same targets could be more easily decimated by drones and ICBM's, with no immediate risk of American lives.

In 2014, in preparation for withdrawal, America destroyed ordinance based in Afghanistan that was of sufficient value to fully fund medical care for all of its citizens. Nothing has changed since Jeffrey Simon made his 1968 comment. If America is to avoid being the 'Babylon the great city' mentioned in *Revelation*, it has got to begin to think smart about the way it exerts influence.

The prophecy calls for the fall of 'Babylon The Great City,' it therefore falls upon elements of American society to clearly ensure that Washington conforms to an analogues image. Thereafter, we are told that 'Babylon that great city has fallen, "having made all nations to drink of the wine of the wrath of her fornication." [14:8]

That image of 'wine' is interesting – in 6:6 we were told not to hurt the 'wine', and later it is associated with the divine 'wrath' – so that 2007 transition to commerce is associated with consistent behavior which in no way damages the reliance on oil, or the basis for divine wrath ... which is in the context of commerce.

The Crimea has spurred talk of expelling Russia from the Group of 8 – an informal organization composed of the United States, Britain, Canada, France, Germany, Italy, Japan, and Russia which meets annually to discuss matters of global importance. If Russia is expelled, the Group of 8 becomes even less relevant on the global stage; moreover, it will have expelled its 2014 chairman at the precise point in history where a routine forum for international discussion is most needed.

If Washington falls, the prophecy is fulfilled; if Moscow falls, the prophecy is fulfilled. Prophecy is not concerned with specifics about those who fulfill its predicted pattern – all that is important is that the pattern conforms to some entity perceived to have global or mystical importance. Historically, Babylon fell to the Persian, Cyrus the Great, then his successor, Darius the Great, was defeated by the Scythians who owned the region of the Crimea and southern Ukraine. That is the historical allusion which is coming into play.

If the prophecy were to be fulfilled in a literal manner, than Iran (ancient Persia) is the one to fall. If we look to a symbolic aggressor – naturally the United States has worked hard to fulfill that role, but Russia also qualifies. Toss in the dragon symbol and you can offer up China as the Babylon – but, Beijing isn't part of the 2013-2014 game; still, the timeline calls for an event in 2015.

Kevin Freeman, a global financial analyst with expertise in financial warfare and terrorism, has pointed out that Russia's best weapon is the American Dollar – especially if they are allied with China, and can create an alternative to the International Monetary Fund and World Bank.

Freeman has stated: "The real risk is if we go after them with economic weapons, they come back after us and this creates World War III." So far as weapons go, China was the original source of paper currency and imposed it on all those who entered the Spice Trade. What is the modern equivalent of the ancient Spice Road? What global consumer products are currently originating in China?

Putin knows the game, and has indicated his belief that the United States is living way beyond its means and has be hedging its economic problems into the world economy, in the same way that high risk mortgages were bundled into bonds and contributed to the 2007 economic turmoil – in that analogy, America is parasitically living off the global economy through a dollar based monopoly.

Putin understands that, if Russia is forced to shift all of its Treasury bond holdings out of the Fed and into offshore accounts, it will be able to freely buy or sell its portfolio in response to any of the threatened economic sanctions over Ukraine. The hard reality remains: the United States needs Russia and China, along with any economically significant nations they influence, to underwrite the huge tax writeoffs provided to the 'Elite' upper one-percent of the American society.

There is a certain humor inherent in the Crimean nonsense.

America, the bastion of Democracy, is challenging the will of an established – allegedly autonomous – Republic as expressed by the ballots of 97-percent of those who chose to vote in what was a hastily called, but open, election in response to the violent actions of "Euromaidan." As a bastion of Capitalism, America now relies on Communist and Socialist nations to provide its consumer goods and underwrite its economic largess.

America, the bastion of 'Christianity,' struggles to deny every premise of Christian Doctrine outlined in scripture. Moreover, the more opposition expressed, the more traditionally Conservative are those representing that opposition; and the more consistent their behavior is with the negative aspects of prophecy.

The Red Horseman, with power to take peace from the earth, confronts the Red States which are striving to exercise that power through irrational militaristic priorities which, in 2012, inspired 173 members of the Republican controlled House of Representatives to urge Defense Secretary Leon Panetta, supporting their decision to produce more tanks, despite the fact that there were 2000 Abrams tanks stored in the American desert which the Secretary wished to refurbish in expectation of a significant 2015 technological change.

Day, Year, Reality
Does the Hour matter

In response to the imposition of sanctions, one Russian who was included – Deputy Prime Minister Dmitry Rogozin – tweeted: *"Comrade Obama, what should those who have neither accounts nor property abroad do? Have you not thought about it?"*
"I think the decree of the President of the United States was written by some joker."
If military action is excluded as a rational possibility, than the point made by DPM Rogozin is valid and originates from a man who grew-up in nation which was economically isolated for forty-five years, and still managed to become an economic force within twenty years of that situation ending – taking less than ten years to be added to the Group of 8 (G8), only to be expelled in March 2014.

The US Federal Reserve Chair Janet Yellen has indicated US interest rates could start to rise in early 2015 – an end of Fed bond purchases near the end of 2014 would imply rate increases around April 2015.

The 2007 joining of the White and Pale Horsemen triggered a global financial crisis which was countered by Federal Reserve action to lower overnight interest rates to zero-percent. In addition, in an attempt to keep long-term borrowing costs low, the central bank started buying bonds.

In part, the objective was to encourage businesses to borrow and spend more – to enhance deficit, or leverage, driven growth – in an effort to spur economic growth and create more jobs. But this is balanced by a political environment striving to deplete disposable income by retaining a sub-poverty minimum wage, combined with a reduction in food stamp and other compensatory assistance.

Meantime, as some had predicted, the self-induced economic crisis depressed growth and countered the demographic pressures which should have increased employment opportunities as the last of the 'Silent Generation' and first of the 'Baby-boomers' moved into retirement.

Demographically speaking, the nation should have seen entry level employment opportunities opening as 'Tweeners' moved up the corporate and industrial ladder. Instead they were faced with high levels of unemployment and a generation of college graduates who are underemployed. But, with the proposal to privatize Social Security, both the 'Tweeners' and the older 'Generation X' crowd were put on notice – the voice announcing the intent to "cast them into the great winepress of the wrath," and Babylon would neither hurt the oil nor the wine of wrath – but would pour it out upon the world.

In keeping with the economic interpretation of 'fornication' imposed by Babylon (Washington), since the 2007 financial crisis, the public debt of the United States government has reached $17.4 trillion – roughly America's annual GDP – with the dollar weakened through the Fed's action of adding $1 trillion into the economy in an effort to spur lending and domestic debt.

In Congress, The Tea Party Movement has made a concerted effort to impose gridlock and hampered efforts to bring the fiscal house into anything resembling order.

Traditional economic theory predicts these actions should cause a decline in the value and importance of the dollar; instead it has held, and even strengthened slightly against the Swiss franc, the Japanese yen, the British pound, and Euro – primarily due to the fact that international trade and financial exchanges are transacted in dollars. Globally, nearly two-thirds of Central bank assets are held in dollar-denominated foreign-currency reserves composed of US Treasury securities.

As shown by the decade it took for the US Dollar to surpass the British pound sterling as the world's main reserve currency, if the "wine of wrath" is to turn to blood, than the media is unlikely to notice it before 2017 (if the Crimea marks the starting date, 2024).

If we think in terms of possible symbolism, than this verse becomes rather interesting [14:20]:

And the winepress was trodden without the city, and blood came out of the winepress, unto the horse bridles, by the space of a thousand and six hundred furlongs.

• The distance of 1600 furlongs is equivalent to approximately 200 miles – which happens to be the approximate distance between the city lines of New York City and Washington, DC; and roughly the distance from the Crimean city of Osovyny (on the Sea of Azov, at the Strait of Kerch, and the Black Sea resort city of Mayak, on the coast directly across Crimea).

• If we read 'wine' as money (root of all evil [1 Timothy 6:10]), than the 'winepress' would be a printing press, or American Federal Reserve – which creates money by buying back its own Treasury Securities.

• The 'horse bridles' would be the horses of war, or those of the Four Horseman.

Because the dollar represents the reserve currency, in self-defense (against any secondary effects from American policies) the central banks of other nations have been storing money in American assets. We must protect, avoid harming, the oil and the money – in the context of either 9/11, the 2014 Crimea situation, or both, being span of the splash.

Remember, the voice proclaimed a warning:

"A measure of wheat for a penny, and three measures of barley for a penny, and oil, and wine hurt thou not."

At the critical point, the price of wheat is three times that of barley – in February 2014 the price per ton of Wheat was $292, and that of Barley $163. It would appear, on the American commodities exchange, the critical criteria had not been reached in February.

But what will happen if an oil pipeline were to contaminate the watertable in a wheat producing region? And some might find it interesting that a major wheat producing region for Russia lies on the eastern shore region of the Sea of Azov and throughout Crimea.

The American President announced his sanctions, those who have no responsibilities in the matter – nor are likely to gain any – are undoubtedly going to escalate the pre-midterm election rhetoric and thereby undermine American credibility. There is a very real possibility that certain politicians will ratchet up the rhetoric about freedom and democracy, which achieved very little during the Cold War era and, given the west is ignoring what appears to be a valid democratic vote, their rhetoric undermines democracy.

The situation in the Ukraine is transient and ultimately will be forgotten. It is of far less global importance than the social breakdowns in Africa and South America – which receive minimal media attention.

Logistically the pattern of events is interesting: In 1994, the Ukraine cancels the Crimean Constitution and its rights as a free Republic; in 2013, the Ukrainian President Viktor Yanukovych's abandoned an EU deal; questionable elements revolt and chase Yanukovych from the country; post Crimea succession, the EU and Ukraine enter into a signed an agreement forging closer economic ties; finally, EU leaders have also agreed to try to reduce energy dependence on Russia – 30-percent of natural gas energy, and 10-percent of EU total energy, are obtained from Russia.

On the Russian side, the Crimean people voted to rejoin Russia, and President Putin signed a law formally absorbing Crimea into Russia. America is free to reject a democratic process, just as hawkish elements are free to replicate the infamous *Charge of the Light Brigade*, using a modern technology, or methodologies draw from a modern economic equivalent of wheat and barley pricing.

Neither America or Europe has any intention of engaging in a military response to the transient Crimea crisis – especially since such action would only serve to destroy global stability, and fulfill one possible interpretation of the prophecy included in the *Book of Revelation*.

It is interesting that fulfillment of prophecy is in the hands of people who specialize in hyperbole and hypocrisy. The honest thing for Western leaders to do is allow the Ukraine to get its house in order. As of this writing, they are do to have an election in May 2014, which has the potential for establishing a valid government.

As the fictional character, Captain Jack Sparrow said: "The

problem is not the problem, the problem is your attitude about the problem." Or more aptly, the prophecy is just reporting how the Red voter will address the prediction taken from the book they love to utilize when justifying their destructive behavior.

The Book of Revelation is a Jewish Prophecy which deals with the reality of predicable Gentile behavior.

In essence, it is a Jewish curse. ... A curse upon those who could be relied upon to insult Jews and whatever deity – the self-begotten beginning – which must have existed before the Big Bang.

Creationists argue the literalist nature of the Bible, with its commandment to abstain from the consumption of pork and shell fish. They often do it over Church pork and bean suppers, or pork chops, or pork roast.

Some Imams teach that the Qur'an teaches as the mediaeval Christians believed – the earth is the center of the alleged 'solar system'. But, like the Bible, the Qur'an agrees with modern science; that does not mean those who take it upon themselves to mislead others will not subvert. Even when the book tells its believers:

"And no question do they bring to you but We reveal to you
the truth and the best explanation" [Qur'an 25:33]

Look at those works, "the truth and the best explanation." If we say, "The sky is blue," we speak the truth – when there are no clouds and when it is daylight. At night, a cloudless sky is clear and colorless. The truth is conditional – especially when it is combined with the words "best explanation."

When the "best explanation" is the one tailored to a limited mentality; the inconsistencies speak to the target audience which is programmed to accept them and not look beyond them to factual differences. Consider these verses from the Qur'an, and apply the logic in other places – remember, everything is the same, they just change the name – some believe, because the term 'Day' is used, they contradict each other as to what a divine day is.

A day in the sight of the Lord is like a thousand years of your reckoning. [22:47]

To Him, on a Day, the space whereof will be a thousands

years of your reckoning. [32:5]

The angels and the spirit ascend unto him in a day the measure whereof is Fifty thousands years. [70:4]

A divine day is like a thousand years on earth – that comes straight out of the Bible. But most of the basics in the Qur'an were taken from the Hebrew Bible. Other words come from the teachings of the Apostles – who were themselves devout Jews and taught in terms of the Hebrew teachings which the Davidic Prophecy said would be either recognized, adopted, or acknowledged, by everyone on the planet.

So, if you have a problem with verse 22:47, you also have a serious problem with the Abrahamic Scriptures – and probably also the very existence of a self-begotten beginning which explains the Big Bang; and, because the Big Bang is an integral part of modern physics , that means you deny the daily physical realities of life. A denial for which, like The Tea Party on Obamacare, you have no substitute to offer – beyond an absolute denial of everything.

Obviously, verse 32:5 simply repeats 22:47, which is an expression of Psalm 90:4,

"A thousand years in your sight are like a day that has just gone by, or like a watch in the night."

As many know, the phrase from Psalms, as repeated in the Qur'an, appears in 2 Peter 3:8 as.

"With the Lord a day is like a thousand years, and a thousand years are like a day."

A passing point being that there is no foundational difference between the three religions, and that any difference in perspective is on the part of the listener – the audience being addressed – and not the teachings themselves, which the listener is supposed follow.

But, back to the differences in verses as generated by 70:4.

Her the operative focus should not be on the measure of a day, but on the fact that it is measured as *"The angels and the spirit ascend."* When ascending the Divine Day reference is different.

We measure a day by our journey around our own axis – by the spin of the earth and the changing exposure to the sun.

The Qur'an and Bibles (Hebrew and Gentile) each express a divine day and an Earth day. The Gentile seems to count a 24-hour day; the Hebrew references daylight hours and the night watch – which raises the question of whether it is referring to a Divine Day in terms of a twelve hour period.

Things can get very confusing and confrontational – yet not shift in terms of the accuracy of the original speech.

This is a problem confronting us with Apocalyptic Prophecy.

The only thing we can state is that we are dealing with two periods of one thousand years each – a period supposedly measured from the perspective of an earth year. Imagine if it were counted in terms of a Divine Year (365,242.5 earth years +/-); that would mean we have seven or eight million years of this nonsense to go.

Think of the evolution which life-forms will undergo during that time. Think of what will happen to those who reject evolution, science, physics, and all the technological and medical discoveries they necessitate. And all because they choose to think 'Day' rather than 'Ascend', and cannot separate the difference between a 'Divine Day' and an earth bound one. Imagine the problems they'll have if humanity ever colonizes the planets and begins to speak of days relative to the colonies.

NO! We cannot know the exact day and hour of whatever the prophecy predicted. But we can, as has been done, look at possible scenarios based upon our concept of days and years – along with those we know to have been used in structuring the patriarch ages to create a readable dating structure for historic points.

The Apocalyptic Prophecy says we are there, and have been for several generations, with the United States defining events.

If the prophecy is correct, and utilizes our standard years, it follows that we are now making the decision as to who will survive and who will die. More important, the decision will involve lots of basic philosophical differences being resolved in a manner which will yield a single society of inter-dependant cultures.

Those who insist everyone else is wrong, and justify their belief by waving their respective scriptures, will either learn that they are the same scripture rephrased, or will die.

Humanity will continue; the earth will continue to rotate and revolve around the sun; the sun will continue to revolve around the point in the universe that serves as its loci; and that is moving to wherever the expansion will take it. But none of that matters if we decide we want to be the victims of prophecy and aide in the spilling of Seven Vials of Wrath.

In accordance with the dating chart which opens our third chapter, the Red Horseman controls events which coincide with America's 2014 Midterm and the 2016 Presidential elections; since 2007, heeding 'a voice', the Pale Horseman has decreed economics to be the battleground.

The 2016 Presidential election will need to face the reality that infrastructure and commodities become less dominant as the related economies get richer.

For the first thirty years of the last century, new fortunes in America were built in retailing and automobiles, amassing wealth from oil wildcatting and railroads belonged to the 19th century.

In 'Red' China the real money comes from the internet, not heavy industry leveraged with subsidized loans against land. There are enormous profits to be made from manufacturing, but what is made is hi-tech computer, hence internet, related. In the modern Chinese world, corruption can not be tolerated in the same way it was only a few decades ago. The government, and businesses have come to recognize that reform and tackle vested interests are better insulated against transient fluctuations in financial markets.

The 'Reds' – Red China, Russia and America's Republicans – are now uniformly representative of various aspects of the global Capitalist reality. The differences come in several ways, first is their attitude toward the average lower class worker, who is expected to move up into the middle-class and grow the economy more.

It is understood that regulating monopolies, and promoting competition, is incompatible with transparency and bribe-takers in a culture composed of a new, educated, urban, taxpaying middle class of the type which arose in America prior to 1929 and arrival of the First Horseman, whose ride lasted from 1931 to 2008, which we can now put on three generations – sins of the fathers to the third and fourth generation type stuff [Deuteronomy 5:9].

When we pass the 76-year mark, we have Millennials who are the tech savvy, well-educated, underemployed twenty-something generation facing the prospect of having a lower standard of living than their parents – all because policies and animosities set down by the Silent Generation have yet to pass into history.

We are witnessing the animosities, the reliance on terms like "socialist" to trigger a knee-jerk Boomer response implanted in the days of "duck-and-cover" when the word "god" became a political tool to distinguish 'them' from 'us', rather than a common point of reference to that self-begotten beginning which helped explain how something of pure energy and intelligence emerged from absolute nothing.

There was a subconscious Pavlovian link created between the term "socialist" and a concept called Mutually assured destruction – it was *MAD(ness)*, conceptually as mad as the 2013 government Shutdown because a small group failed, having brought it to a vote 42 time, to deny the very-poorest of working Americans access to privatized healthcare insurance.

By denial of affordable coverage, a member of the working poor, who becomes sick, loses work, goes on Medicaid/Medicare and related public assistance. Aside from decreasing the Tax rolls, it increases deficits. Anyone who claims to want to reduce deficits is acting in a way that is *MAD(ness)*. In effect, it invokes another relic of the 'Cold War' – The Domino Theory, one stupidity creates a series of unwanted consequences which reach fruition in 2015.

The Silent Generation became so enamored with either the process of either inserting "god" into everything, or avoiding the topic to the point of removing religion from life, that the concept of "divine" almost vanished – but was forced back into life by Hippy Flower-Power and the power of acceptance which has finally taken root. With acceptance comes changes in laws and return of a loving Genesis deity – neither named nor confined to fixed structures.

The last vestige of the White Horseman can be seen in the politicized stresses on the social safety net aimed at breaking faith with the post-war generations, while destroying the resources which should be safeguarded – the vials of wrath are being poured on the ground, into the water, and sprayed into the air. This action is not a divine wrath, but the last vindictive action of jealous wrath by a destructive generation whose only measure of worth is its power to kill.

Every day, over 10,000 Boomers retire as they are confronted by a doomed political class seeking to privatize their only reliable monthly check and the cornerstone of their financial preparation.

In 2014 and 2016, the American voter will determine if their nation, their capital, the Washington DC, is Babylon the great city and whether or not it will fall. If it does, it falls at their hands, and their hands alone. Prophecy does not care who fulfills it – only that it be fulfilled on schedule, and that the fulfillment can only be seen retroactively.

For the very few who actually believe in their documents of the religion; and the fewer still who actually understand them, the game is a spectator sport, the outcome of which is already certain – they will sit in the stands, cheer their respective teams, and then go home. Hopefully, the game will have been interesting and they will not have dropped any food or drink on their clothes.

In terms of *Revelation*, the author is betting on *MAD* – the consistent pattern of America Right-Wing politics has been to shoot itself in the foot of its constituents. *Revelation* tells us they will first go into shock, a number of them will bleed to death and the rest ... we have no idea. But, we do know that a third of the population is predicted to perish, and, so long as their constituency does not exceed its current numbers – which happens to be about a third of voters, it really isn't relevant.

The Timeline indicates Hitler was governed by a Horseman of Divine Wrath – indirectly an agent of "god" – obviously selected to gather *The Chosen* before the real horrors began. If voted more power, "*Red*" take peace from the earth – 2014/15/16 decides.

www.ingramcontent.com/pod-product-compliance
Lightning Source LLC
Chambersburg PA
CBHW060421290526
45791CB00002B/842